Paris by Plaque

MONTMARTRE

by

Anna Meakin

&

Paul Bethel

Translation by Peter Clare

Counting House Books

London | Paris

First published 2011 by Counting House Books Ltd
www.countinghousebooks.com
info@countinghousebooks.com

London & Paris

ISBN 978-095676-140-8

Paris By Plaque
Montmartre

parisbyplaque.com

1 2 3 4 5 6 7 8 9 10

Book design by Chris Sims

Printed in the United Kingdom

Paris By Plaque

Montmartre

Respirer Paris, cela conserve l'âme…
To breathe Paris preserves the soul…

Victor-Marie Hugo
Les Misérables, vol.3, bk.1, ch.6.

Contents

How to use this book

Paris by Plaque provides translations of the *Histoire de Paris* plaques and an exploration of their historical context, along with three mapped walks so that you can visit every site. The plaques, designed by Philippe Starck and installed by the Mayor of Paris in 1993 are an elegant, unobtrusive and eco-friendly addition to the streets of Paris. They are fondly regarded by Parisians, and the Mayor himself.

In this first book of the series we cover the plaques in the 18th *arrondissement*, or district. Most of them are in and around the hill-top village of Montmartre, or the *Butte* as it is often known.

The first italicised and indented paragraph of each chapter is a translation of the French text on the plaques. An explanation of the text and illustrations follows.

The plaques are numbered and listed alphabetically by French title. Throughout the book we cross-reference related plaques with their number in brackets, so that you can connect the stories together.

Short accounts of The Siege of Paris and the Commune are included, which may help those unfamiliar with this important period of the city's history to understand the plaques more fully.

The walks, which visit a majority of the plaques, are split into three. They also connect, so that you can either do each one individually, or carry on and do more than one in a day. The timings below are approximate for a leisurely paced walk and do not include time you may spend exploring the locations. Each walk has its own map.

> Walk One is 30 minutes
> Walk Two is 1 hour and 30 minutes
> Walk Three is 40 minutes

There are also maps to help you locate the six outlying plaques that are not on the walks.

At the back of the book is a very basic timeline. A Connections Map shows that Montmartre was primarily a village community, and how the close links between the buildings and characters in its history reflect that.

Please visit the Paris by Plaque website for more photographs and historical background.

www.parisbyplaque.com

We hope you enjoy exploring Montmartre and reading the stories hidden in the historical plaques.

The Siege & Commune

The Siege of Paris

In July 1870, Napoleon III declared war on the Kingdom of Prussia. It was a disastrous decision and he was forced to surrender and abdicate as Emperor less than two months later. His defeat and the capture of an entire French army at the Battle of Sedan was a national humiliation. The Prussians, led by Otto von Bismark, were set to invade France but the citizens of Paris refused to accept defeat. On learning of Napoleon's capture they overthrew the government – the French Second Empire – abolished the monarchist structure and replaced it with the Government of National Defence. General Louis Jules Trochu, Jules Favre and Léon Gambetta led the coup.

Meanwhile, the Prussian army surrounded Paris and dug in leaving the occupants cut off. No-one could enter or leave the city and soon the population began to starve. Léon Gambetta left Paris on his famous balloon trip **(1)** to summon help from Tours. At his urging all remaining French troops marched towards Paris in order to attack the Prussians from every side. The citizens of the capital were required to form a military 'home guard', named the *francs-tireurs*.

As winter set in food shortages worsened. Parisians resorted to eating dogs, cats and rats – anything in fact – to avoid starvation. Some astonishingly inventive menus from the time have survived, showing how imaginative chefs attempted to make restaurant dishes of rat and cat sound appealing. Even the city's zoo animals were not spared, including the famous elephants, Castor and Pollux. They were shot and bought by M. Deboos, an enterprising butcher who declared them a delicacy and sold

Gruesome scenes at a street butcher during the Siege

trunk at forty-five francs a pound, despite the fact it was said to be all but inedible. It was not only food that was scarce. Parisians tore up the benches from the streets and felled trees for fuel as the temperature plummeted.

The Prussians eventually forced a surrender following a sustained three-week bombardment of the capital, which began late on the 27th December. Jules Favre secretly negotiated an armistice with the Prussians at Versailles. It was estimated that during the four months of the Siege 65,000 people perished.

The Prussians demanded a victory parade through the capital which Adolphe Thiers, leader of the National Assembly, agreed to in exchange for France retaining the city of Belfort. However, he was forced to capitulate on the annexation of the territories of Alsace and most of Lorraine which infuriated his political opponents. The Prussians confiscated most of the National Guards' weapons and demanded to station their troops in the major Paris forts until two hundred million francs had been paid in ransom.

The anger and shock felt by Parisians at the terms of this humiliating surrender sowed the seeds of the insurrection that followed, culminating in the Paris Commune.

The Paris Commune

The Commune of 1871 had a deep and lasting impact upon the people of Paris. It began in Montmartre, following the Siege, when government troops tried to sieze artillery back from the people. The cannons had been paid for by ordinary working Parisians to defend themselves against the Prussians. The people, furious at the terms of surrender that the Government of National Defence had conceded, refused to give up their weapons. After the turbulent events that followed (9 & 27), a socialist republic was proclaimed in the city, called *La Commune*. Marx sat in London and looked on, whilst the Communards siezed the Government headquarters at the Hôtel du Ville. Thier's government fled to Versailles. The suddenness of the uprising surprised even the insurgent leaders, and there was some disarray as they planned their next move.

It was an important time of social change. Women played a critical role in the Commune, fighting alongside men on the barricades. They organised hospitals, ambulances, schools and food distribution depots. They also set up a garment depository from where the poor were clothed. As in subsequent wars, women's emancipation was pushed forward during the ten weeks of the Commune. In fact, one of the most fervent fighters and organisers of the uprising was a woman called Louise Michel (32).

Social conditions also improved. Decrees were issued banning all-night working for bakers. Tools pawned during the Siege by desperate workers were returned so that they could finally begin to trade again.

Thiers did not to tolerate the uprising for

The Communards in Père Lachaise Cemetery

long, however. Troops retook the city district by district, with savage fighting leaving

Troops search for insurgents during 'Bloody Week'

thousands of dead and wounded on both sides. Paris herself was a victim, as the Communards set fire to many important buildings as they felt the Versaillais close in. Notre Dame Cathedral was saved at the last moment, but Communards murdered the Archbishop of Paris in a needless act of brutality.

The final battles took place at night in the cemeteries of Montmartre and Père Lachaise. In the latter, the Communards' Wall, or *Mur des Fédérés*, commemorates the spot where one hundred and forty seven of the last remaining Communards were lined up and executed. Many Parisians still visit the site to pay their respects.

Government retribution was merciless after the crushing of the Commune. In what was to

become known as the *Semaine Sanglante*, or Bloody Week (21st to the 28th May 1871), the brutality of the backlash was truly horrifying. Troops checked the palms of citizens' hands for gunpowder traces, which they took as an sign of treason. Vengeance was swift and, in many cases, suspects were shot on the spot.

Historians estimate the number of Parisians killed for taking part in the uprising was around 20,000. Women were put firmly back in their place, with hundreds of deportations and executions. It was a terrible and bloody chapter in the history of the city, which left deep scars. People would begin to question not only the ruling establishment, but also the very nature of nationalism itself.

The Walks

Walk One

About ½ mile; approximate duration – 30 minutes

- Begin at metro Abbesses. The entrance of the metro is one of only two glass canopied entrances that remain in Paris, designed in the fluid Art Nouveau style by Hector Grimauld in 1900.

- Bear slightly right, and cross the street to find **(2) Église Saint-Jean-l'Évangéliste** outside the church.

- Return past the metro to walk along rue Yvonne le Tac (the middle street). On your right you will pass **(36) Naissance de la Compagnie de Jésus**. The crypt is open every Friday between 3.00pm and 6.00pm.

- At the end of rue Yvonne le Tac, turn left in to rue des Trois Frères, and walk uphill to the bend, where you will find **(21) Le Dispensaire de Clemenceau**.

- Retrace your steps down rue Les Trois Frères and continue downhill to place Dullin and **(30) Le Théâtre de l'Atelier**.

- Carry on down rue Dancourt past *Le Bon Bock* restaurant (est. 1879) and arrive at boulevard de Rochechouart.

- Turn left and find **(18) Le Chat Noir** next to No. 84 and **(3) L'Élysée Montmartre** along this road.

- Turn right up rue Steinkerque. Arrive at **(1) Départ en Ballon de Gambetta**.

  If you feel like extending this walk, **(7) La Colline au Néolithique** is just to your right, and **(31) Les Grands Magasins Dufayel** is in the same direction, roughly ten minutes walk away – see separate maps. Afterwards, retrace your steps back to the top of rue Steinkerque.

- Continue along place Saint Pierre.

At this point, you may either walk along rue Tardieu to return to Abbesses metro, or take the next right into place Suzanne Valadon and proceed to the funicular to continue with Walk 2.

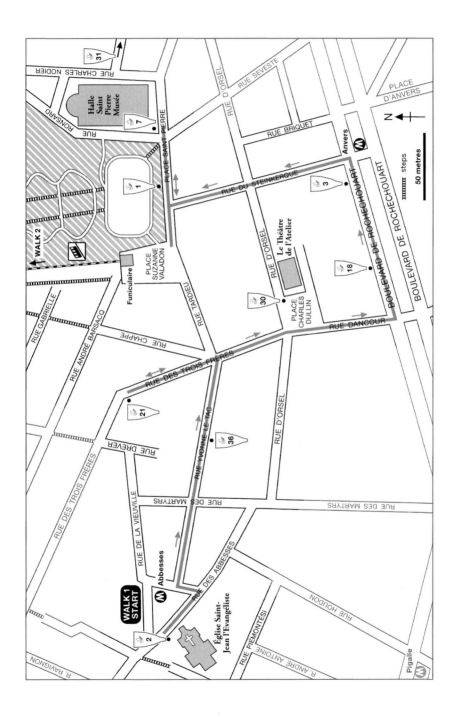

Walk Two

About 1½ miles; approximate duration – 1 hour and 30 minutes

If you are starting with this walk, go to the nearest metro (Anvers) and walk up rue de Steinkerque, turn left into place Saint Pierre and take the next right into place Suzanne Valadon to arrive at the foot of th funicular. If you are continuing from Walk One, start here.

- Ascend by the funicular to Sacré Cœur. Turn right as you exit the funicular and walk down rue du Cardinal Dubois. Note spectacular views across Paris to the right. Walk up the steps in front of Sacré-Cœur, and turn left at the top. At the beginning of rue Azaïs, find **(6) La Basilique du Sacré-Cœur** on your left, by the fence.

- Carry on along rue Azaïs and find **(14) La Statue du Chevalier de la Barre** on the left, by square Nadar. Opposite find **(27) Le Parc d'artillerie de Montmartre**.

- Turn right on to rue Saint Éleuthère and find **(33) Mairie du Montmartre** on the left. Turn to face the right and you will see **(37) Saint-Pierre de Montmartre** in place Jean Marais.

- Proceed down rue Norvins, which runs along the top of place du Tertre. Carry on down rue Norvins, passing *Le Consulat* restaurant on the right hand side. Continue down rue Norvins to find **(8) La Folie Sandrin** on the right.

- Look behind you and you will see **(13) La Mire du Nord** beside the old boulangerie *Le Fournil du Village*, which has been the communal bakery for years.

- Retrace your steps to *Le Consulat* restaurant, then turn immediately left, past the historic *La Bonne Franquette* restaurant, and continue down rue des Saules. **(12) La Maison Rose de Maurice Utrillo** is on your left, just past the junction. Turn into rue Cortot across the road, where you will find **(11) La Maison de Rose de Rosimond**, now the Museum of Montmartre. Walk along rue Cortot, past the water tower and right into rue Mont Cenis

- Turn left down rue du Chevalier de la Barre where you will have some wonderful views of the back of Sacré Cœur. Find **(9) Fusillade du 18 Mars 1871** on the left before the corner.

- Ahead is the parc de la Turlure. Enter the park and proceed to the waterfall. If you look back at Sacré-Cœur from here, on top of one of the domes you can see a hidden green bronze statue of Saint Michel slaying a dragon.

- Exit the park at the bottom, on to rue de la Bonne, then continue down the hill, bearing left into rue St Vincent. On the corner of rue Becquerel, find **(32) Louise Michel directrice d'école**, which is outside her first school.

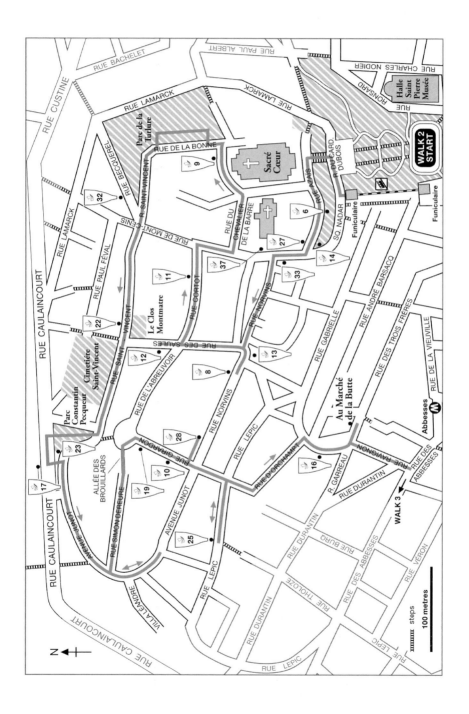

- Proceed along rue St Vincent, past the nature garden and *Le Clos Montmartre* vineyard. Look up left over the vines to see the back of the Museum of Montmartre. Find **(22) Le Lapin Agile** on the right, where rue des Saules joins rue St Vincent.

- Continue down rue St Vincent until you reach place Constantin Pecqueur. Enter the park to see a statue dedicated to Steinlen. This is the site of Montmare's old *abreuvoir,* or watering hole. Exit the park at the bottom, and turn left along rue Caulaincourt, past the statue of Symbolist artist Eugène Carrière. Cross the road to see **(17) Le Cat's Cottage de Steinlen.** Sadly the cottage itself is no longer visible.

- Cross the road and pass **(23) Le Maquis** at the end of avenue Junot. Walk up avenue Junot, noting the Art Nouveau architecture, being sure to visit the charming Villa Léandre on your right.

- Pause to see 'The Witches Rock' in the alley next to No. 15 before walking back down the hill to rue Simon Dereure, now on the right hand side.

- Continue along rue Simon Dereure to place Casadesus, and climb the steps into allée des Brouillards. Glimpse Le Château des Brouillards on your right. At the end of the alley, turn right into rue Girardon where you will find **(19) Le Château des Brouillards.**

- Continue up rue Girardon and find **(10) La Légende de Saint Denis** on the right hand side. Explore the park if you have time. Carry on up rue Girardon until you reach place Aymé which is on your left: here you will find **(28) Le Passe-Muraille.** Carry on down rue Girardon, past the tiny *Cine 13.*

- Turn right into rue Lepic. Proceed down rue Lepic to find **(25) Le Moulin de la Galette** on the right hand side. Cross over to the top of rue Tholoze for a better view of the entrance and the windmill above. Behind you is a view of the golden dome of Les Invalides in the distance.

- Retrace your steps up rue Lepic on the right hand side of the road. When you come to rue d'Orchampt, turn round and look up at the more modern windmill above the Moulin de la Galette restaurant. Walk down rue d'Orchampt, passing the singer Dalida's house on the right hand side. At the end of the road, turn right into place Émile Goudeau to find **(16) Le Bateau-Lavoir.**

- Walk downhill to the end of place Émile Goudeau and continue down the steps.

  If you enjoyed the film *Amélie* you may like to turn left after descending the steps. Walk a short distance down rue des Trois Frères on your left to find the grocer shop that featured as 'Maison Collignon' in the film.

- Walk along rue Ravignan to rue des Abbesses. *At this point, you may either turn left back to Abbesses metro, or turn right to continue with Walk 3.*

Walk Three

About ¾ mile; approximate duration – 40 minutes

If you are starting with this walk, go to the nearest metro (Abbesses) and turn right at the exit to walk along rue des Abbesses. If you are continuing from Walk II, start here.

- Continue along rue des Abbesses. At the junction with rue Tholoze, glance right for a last view of the Le Moulin de la Galette.

- Turn left down rue Lepic, then turn right into rue Constance. At the end you will cross over to Impasse Marie Blanche, where you will find **(5) L'hôtel du Compte de L'Escalopier.**

The plaque itself in on the left; but continue to the end of impasse Marie Blanche where, on the right-hand side, you will find Maison Eymonaud, believed to be partly constructed from the remains of the original L'Escalopier's mansion. (Go past the two No. 7's and ignore the "Privé" sign.) This house is open to the public (no charge) on Mondays to Fridays between 10.00am and 4.00pm during July, August and up to 15th September. If it is not open, you can still see some of the ornate carving and stonework through the gate.

- Go down rue Cauchois to return to rue Lepic. Fans of the film *Amélie* will recognise *Café des deux Moulins* on the left-hand corner, where you can buy a crème brûlée named after her.

- Turn right to continue down rue Lepic to boulevard de Clichy, turning right at the bottom towards the Moulin Rouge. Find **(26) Le Moulin Rouge** on the right.

- Continue west along boulevard de Clichy, noting Cité Véron – on your right before arriving at Avenue Rachel. At the far end you will find **(20) Le Cimetière Montmartre.**

- Retrace your steps down rue Rachel and turn right onto boulevard de Clichy.

- At the junction with rue Caulaincourt, outside Castorama, you will find **(4) L'Hippo-Palace.** Inside, at the back of the restaurant, you will find a wall of old photographs showing the Hippo-Palace and the Gaumont Palace.

- Continue down boulevard de Clichy, crossing the road by the historic *Wepler* Restaurant to arrive at **(35) Monument à la Mémoire de Moncey** on the pedestrian island.

Just before you finish the walk at place de Clichy metro, you may care to note the Art Déco restaurant *Le Charlot* on the other side of boulevard de Clichy.

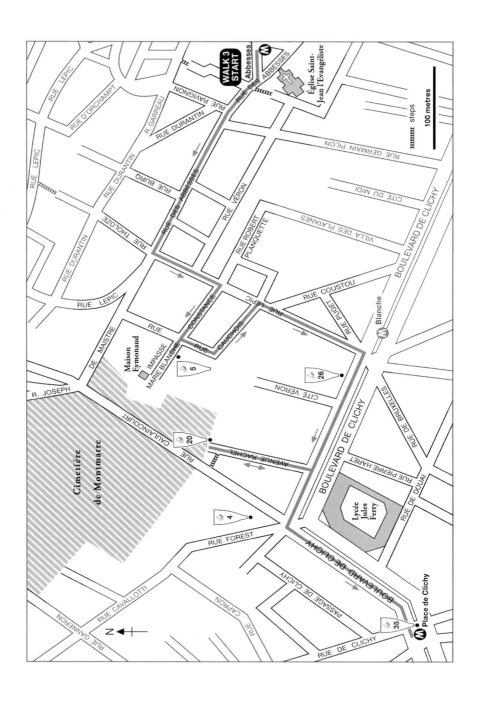

The Remaining Plaques

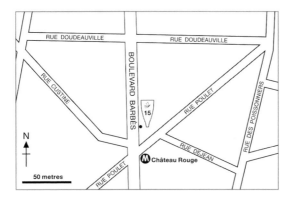

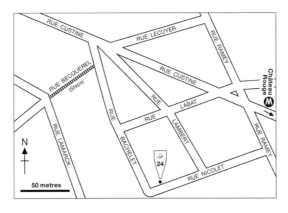

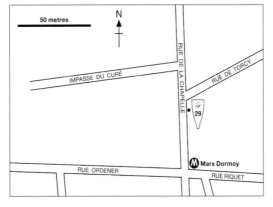

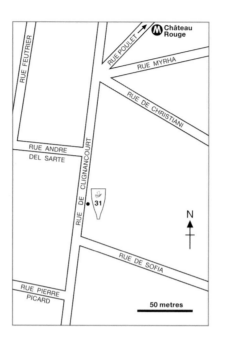

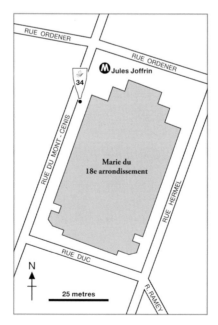

The Plaques

1. Départ en ballon de Gambetta

Gambetta's departure by balloon

In 1870, war and the siege of Paris launched Gambetta's career as an aviator. From 4th September his troupe of balloonists was "revolutionarily" based at place Saint-Pierre. Inaugurated on 23rd September by 'The Neptune', the hot-air balloons were used not only for reconnaissance but also for postal communications. On 7th October a new balloon called the 'Armand-Barbès' carrying Gambetta, then Minister of the Interior of the Government of National Defence, cast off from the middle of a crowd that had come to witness the event. Victor Hugo, a spectator, commented: "The weather was fine, with warming autumn sunshine. Beneath Gambetta's balloon hung a tricolour pennant, while shouts of 'Vive la République!' could be heard."

Paris was under siege, cut off from the outside world by Prussian troops, and nearing starvation. Growing concern about the lack of communication gave rise to a daring plan to escape the city by hot-air balloon. Léon Gambetta needed somehow to reach Tours to plead for government reinforcements. A trial run by experienced balloonist Jules Duruof, in a leaky old craft called *The Neptune*, had proved it was possible – just – and the plan went ahead. The hot-air balloon was now a military utility.

Gambetta arrived for his flight warmly clad in a fur coat and hat, but was pale with nerves as he climbed into the basket in the midst of hundreds of cheering Parisians. The balloon rose, and with it the hopes of the besieged city.

Disaster was narrowly averted when the *Armand Barbès* was fired at as it sank perilously close to the Prussian lines. Gambetta's hand was grazed by a bullet, but the quick thinking pilot jettisoned ballast and the balloon lifted up again and out of danger, eventually landing fifty

Balloon factory, Gare du Nord

miles from Paris at Montdidier. Gambetta's landing was another near disaster. The balloon clipped an oak tree on its descent, nearly pitching him out of the basket. Bruised and shaken he travelled on by train to Tours, and there released a homing pigeon to take news of his success back to the anxiously waiting city.

The military use of balloons in the Paris Siege was 'revolutionary', since it had never before been so effectively employed, or undertaken on such a scale. Teams of seamstresses and rope-makers set about the mass production of balloons in the disused railway stations of the capital. These huge spaces were necessary as full-sized templates were required, and the balloons had to be hung from the iron girders of the station roof to check for leakage. It was traditional for balloons to be made of silk, but since so many were required, and could only make one flight each, the cheapest calico was used instead. This was soaked and ironed before being painted with a mixture of linseed oil and lead oxide to make it airtight. Then, under the watchful eye of Madame Duruof, hundreds of seamstresses pieced the balloons together on sewing machines, rows of which were installed at the Gare du Nord. It was an heroic group effort.

Over the coming months, sixty-six balloons in total escaped Paris, carrying thousands of letters and pigeons. Parisian ingenuity reached new heights during the Siege. Letters were recorded on microfilm, and inserted into the tail feathers of homing pigeons, meaning each bird could carry the equivalent of five thousand messages.

The Prussians retaliated by developing swivel-mounted guns in an attempt to shoot down the balloons, but all efforts failed. The balloonists simply cast off at night to avoid detection. They also used coal gas as fuel, which did not need a flame to reheat it, thus making the balloons virtually undetectable. The Prussians even tried setting hawks on the carrier pigeons to try and halt the flow of information but without success.

2. Église Saint-Jean-l'Évangéliste

The Church of St. John the Evangelist

Petitioned by the priest of the extensive parish of Saint-Pierre de Montmartre, Paris' first modern church was constructed between 1894 and 1904, and was the work of Anatole de Baudot, a student of Henri Labrouste. An original thinker from a strong theoretical background, Baudot was born in Sarrebourg in 1834 and died laden with honours in 1915. He conceived of an architecture shaped by socio-economic factors, in harmony with the advances of the industrial age. The progressive and rational Baudot exerted a strong influence over his students and dared to introduce iron casting and reinforced concrete in his structures. In addition, his publications condemned the camouflaging of materials and structures in buildings. In 1904, the year of the church's inauguration, Baudot published 'Architecture and Reinforced Concrete', a book which records a period of significant development in architecture and research up to the outbreak of the First World War. Even if visitors are still taken aback by this church, sometimes to the point of lively debate, critics commend the originality of the enterprise. The orientalist décor in the 'modern style' contrasts with traditional design of the church, which lies on two levels owing to the steepness of the hill.

Baudot's extraordinary and innovative church is a product of the dogged determination of a certain Abbot Sobaux. The little hill-top church of St Pierre de Montmartre **(37)** was in an advanced state of disrepair, and struggling to house an ever-increasing flock. The Abbot began collecting money from "the whole of Paris!" to fund a new building. The faithful were generous and before long work could begin. Sobaux bought an old orchard in place des Abbesses for the site of the new church, which presented considerable engineering challenges due to the extreme drop in levels. It was at this point that he encountered his first objection. What ensued was a good old-fashioned planning dispute. The City Planning Department refused planning permission, even though St Pierre's was by then closed due to structural instability – in fact it was on the point of total collapse. Sobaux could not change their minds, and finally declared that he would build the church 'as a private citizen', hoping to escape the jurisdiction. In 1897, work began on the foundations. It continued until 1900, when disaster struck: the City Planning Department issued a decree to have the church demolished. But the Abbot's vision would be saved. Whether by divine providence or a quirk of timing, the national scandal of the Dreyfus Affair saw certain legal cases suspended across the city. The decision was reversed just in time and building work could continue. Sobaux had kept his nerve and finally saw his church consecrated in 1904.

The gifted architect Anatole de Baudot was commissioned to design the church, and he set to work using the then revolutionary technique of combining rods and concrete, with an outer skin of brick. Like Saboux, Baudot was also a passionate man. He deplored the "camouflaging" of construction materials, which he saw as reminiscent of the industrial revolution. The visible concrete inside the church is a deliberate architectural statement. While it might sound like a recipe for brute ugliness, the result is striking, with brightly coloured gems of stained glass and mosaic thrown into radiant relief against a dark background of polished concrete.

The Abbot who succeeded Sobaux was Edouard Loutil, also known as Peter the Hermit. He oversaw the decoration of the church with an artist's eye, commissioning the finest sculptors, painters and stained-glass craftsmen. High up are the horsemen of the Apocalypse, and eagles, symbolising St John, are all around. Exquisitely beautiful artworks compete for your attention in this extraordinary church and, although it still divides opinion, there can be no doubt that the vision of Sobaux and Baudot never fails to astonish.

3. L' Élysée Montmartre

The Élysée Montmartre

Opened during the First Empire, its moment of glory arrived with Olivier Metra, who conducted a 40-piece orchestra there. "A double staircase leads us to the Élysée, which is composed of three buildings with a vast, well-stocked garden. The Salon, raised up as if by magic, is second to none, one thousand metres long with no columns; its galleries leading to an immense stone platform where the orchestra is placed; its waterfalls, its plants of every type add still to the enchanting beauty of this great monument". A revolutionary club during the Commune, it lost most of its patrons before making a comeback at the end of the century, with La Goulue and Valentin 'The Boneless' amongst a remarkable company of dancers.

The Élysée Montmartre has reflected shifts in both popular and political culture for over two hundred years. First opened in 1807 as a concert hall, it held genteel musical recitals on its magnificent orchestral stage. The proprietor, M. Adrien Serres, ensured the venue was a huge success by luring conductor Olivier Metra of the rival Bal Mabille to become the leader of the Élysée's orchestra. The Élysée gardens were a big draw too, with paths and groves to wander and a dance area. There was also a covered chalet for when it was cold or wet, which was full of popular games of the day, such as 'Shoot The Bird', and billiards. The Élysée eventually became the most fashionable of the ballrooms that proliferated in Paris in the mid-1800's. There were even ex-army bouncers on the door, armed with swords to keep out the riff-raff.

As the political landscape changed, so did the Élysée. It was closed down during the Siege, when it became a balloon-manufacturing site, under the management of the balloonist Félix Nadar. During the Commune it served as a temporary hospital and revolutionaries' meeting hall. But, despite having lost all its business during these turbulent times, it was the Élysée that caught the wave of the new dance-hall craze that followed. The management sold off the gardens to the Trianon next door, and the Élysée became one of the very first risqué dance-halls for which Paris became so famous. The fashion for the Polka was overtaken by the Can-Can, and it was at the Élysée that the outrageous dancer Louise Weber, nicknamed *La Goulue*, and her bizarrely flexible dance partner Valentin, first made their names.

Artists and writers – never far away in Montmartre – flocked to the venue to experience the new energy that electrified the area at the turn of the century. Toulouse-Lautrec famously painted Louise Weber dancing there, and Zola described it in his best-selling novel *L'Assommoir*, (The Drinking Den) which described the soul-crushing living conditions of the local working-classes. Guy de Maupassant set his short story *The Mask* in the Élysée and his description of a masked ball there gives a flavour of the atmosphere,

"The patrons came from every quarter of Paris; there were people of all classes who love noisy pleasures, a little low and tinged with debauch. There were clerks and girls – girls of every description, some wearing common cotton, some the finest batiste; rich girls, old and covered with diamonds, and poor girls of sixteen, full of the desire to revel, to belong to men, to spend money. Elegant black evening suits, in search of fresh or faded but appetizing novelty, wandering through the excited crowds, looking, searching, while the masqueraders seemed moved above all by the desire for amusement….Already the far-famed quadrilles had attracted around them a curious crowd…two women, whose lower limbs seemed to be attached to their bodies by rubber springs, were making wonderful and surprising motions with their legs..."

The Mask, (1889) Guy de Maupassant

As the century progressed and tastes changed the Élysée Montmartre was forced to rely on other crowd-pullers. It hosted skating events, high-profile boxing matches and film shows. Today, pop concerts have ensured that the venue is as popular as ever. A fire at the building, in March 2011, has left it scarred, but as a historic monument it will be fully restored.

4. L'Hippo-Palace

The Hippodrome

Inaugurated on 13th May 1900 with the magnificent equestrian show 'Vercingétorix', which brought together 200 artists, 50 horses and 6 elephants, the Hippodrome was a grand multi-purpose space. After the horse racing, the football matches and the skating competitions its five thousand spectators could watch film shows. This was its role until 1908 when it became the Hippo-Palace, officially converted on 27th September 1911 by Léon Gaumont as the Parisian temple of the cinema, under the name of the Hippodrome-Gaumont-Palace. In 1917, Erik Satie staged 'Parade' there, the first Cubist spectacle, with designs and costumes by Picasso. A victim of its own enormity, it disappeared in 1973, with only the great organs escaping demolition, which were later re -erected at the Pavilion Baltard.

The Hippodrome's first incarnation was as an equestrian showground, offering Roman chariot races in the heart of Paris. Built in 1900, and able to seat eight thousand spectators, the building was designed by the architects Galeron, Cambon and Duray, in time to capitalise on the influx of visitors to the Great Exhibition.

It was opened with a grand spectacle. Wearing beautifully elaborate costumes, the performers were led into the ring by a charioteer driving what was said to be the Duke of Brunswick's old coach. The show re-enacted the thrilling battle exploits of Vercingétorix, heroic leader of the Gauls.

With stabling for 200 horses and an 84 metre track, the Hippodrome was a huge success. The events were glamorous, fast and dangerous, with beautiful female charioteers risking serious injury on the racetrack. Accidents were a constant anxiety, which added to the thrill. A doctor and veterinary

Hippodrome Poster (1900)

surgeon were permanent employees. Talented equestrienne Céleste Mogador described the perils of being a Hippodrome rider, and detailed the type of spectacle staged by the management. These included mock hunts with stags and hounds, as well as straight steeplechases.

From 1902 the Hippodrome briefly became Circus Bostock, renowned for its performing lions and tigers. There were also a number of peculiarly shaped and gifted performers including tiny Anita 'The Living Doll' and a double-jointed Indian fakir. But the arrival of cinema meant a conversion was inevitable.

In 1911, the Hippodrome achieved fame as the Gaumont Palace, 'Le Plus Grand Cinema du Monde!', (The World's Biggest Cinema!) seating 3,400. It was beautifully illuminated, promising escapism and glamour. Patrons could dine at intimate, dimly lit tables while they watched a film. Carriages packed the streets outside as elegantly attired high-society flocked to the evening glow of the Gaumont,

eager to see the latest release.

The Cubist ballet *Parade* has seldom been re-staged, due perhaps to its extreme oddness. Conceived and written by Jean Cocteau, it caused a riot on one occasion such was the challenge of the piece. Some of the costumes, designed by Picasso, were made out of stiff cardboard, which barely allowed the dancers to move at all.

A radical Art Deco rebuild by the architect Henri Belloc in 1930 followed the introduction of talkies and a magnificent 1,500 pipe organ was installed. The cinema could then hold 6,000, but by 1950 it was unable to sustain itself any longer. The organ survives and is now housed in the Baltard Pavilion just beyond Paris in Nogent-sur-Marne. It remains in perfect working order.

Sadly there is nothing left to see at this site. But, hidden away on a wall at the back of the restaurant in the current building, there are photos and posters from the Hippodrome in its heyday.

The Hippodrome in 1902, hosting Circus Bostock

5. L'hotel du compte de l'Escalopier

The Mansion of Count l'Escalopier

On 9th April 1812 at Liancourt, Picardy, Marie-Joseph-Charles de l'Escalopier was born, a descendant of a noble family. His studies completed, his wealth allowed him to follow the new science of Archaeology, and in 1835 near the district of Barrière Blanche, he ordered the building of a gothic residence, reflecting his taste for the newly popular 'troubadour' style. In the grounds he installed innovative steam-heated greenhouses and a gymnasium, but would soon replace them with a 5,000-volume library and a small museum of medieval goldsmithing. He returned to Liancourt and died there in 1861, bequeathing his collections to the town of Amiens. The mansion was sold and demolished in 1882.

Marie-Joseph-Charles de l'Escalopier was a learned scholar, archaeologist, curator and horticulturalist. It was here, where once open fields stretched out as far as the horizon, that he chose to build his gothic mansion and pursue his passions.

The glass hothouse was a popular feature of many grand establishments in Paris, but few caused as much excitement as the glasshouses within the grounds of the Mansion of Count l'Escalopier. They were landscaped inside, with little pools and streams, allowing visitors to wander amongst the plants. The cutting-edge steam-heating system, the first in the whole of Paris, allowed the Count's collection of rare tropical plants to thrive.

Eleven interconnected glasshouses ran directly from the mansion, and could be accessed via a small sitting-room. Measuring one hundred and twenty feet in length, and built around an iron frame, the hot-houses were breathtaking. The tallest, at twenty eight feet high, "...whose columns [had] gilded capitals..." was dedicated solely to the cultivation of bananas. Planted in the soil of another were bamboo, papaya, breadfruit, rose apple, and coconut palms. In the hottest room of all exquisite orchids, sandalwood, nutmeg, cocoa and vanilla plants flourished.

The Count's skill with plants was matched only by his scholarship. Publishing his first academic work at the age of just twenty-three, he was most admired for his translation of a medieval text by the monk Theophilus. This helped to retrieve lost knowledge about craftsmanship techniques. The book was part of a reawakening of interest in the Middle Ages during the Second Renaissance, and l'Escalopier was awarded the Legion of Honour for his contribution to learning.

The Count's neo-gothic mansion was inspired by this fascination with the art, craft and architecture of the Middle Ages. The 'troubadour' style mirrored the gothic revival in England, and developed out of a rejection of the neo-classical, which had dominated much of European art. It also signalled a reconnection with Christianity, severed during the years of the French Revolution. The mansion was a paean to the Middle Age craftsman, with a "faithful copy of the door of Joan of Arc at Domremy", turrets and crenelations, wooden carvings and stained-glass windows. The little museum that the Count built in the grounds contained rare medieval items including silver, ivories, bronzes, enamels, wood carvings, and relics.

Eventually one obsession overtook the other and the glasshouses were demolished to make way for a vast library. The Count, driven always by deep religious sentiment, travelled to Rome and Jerusalem to obtain rare texts for his collection. His most prized manuscripts, however, was a draft of the abdication of Emperor Napoleon, signed by the man himself.

Sadly, the magnificent mansion did not survive for long. At the age of forty-six the Count became seriously ill and was forced to return to his birthplace at Castle Liancourt. He died two years later. The entire library was bequeathed to the city of Amiens.

By a quirk of fate another neo-gothic building, Maison Eymonaud, is just a few steps away from here, to your right, at No.7 impasse Marie Blanche. Built in the 1890's, it is rumoured that parts of l'Escalopier's mansion were rescued and reused by the architect. Eymonaud was an antique dealer and woodcarver, who housed his workshop and antiques showroom here. A visit might give a flavour of the Count's mansion before it was demolished. It is possible to go inside and look around between July and mid-September. Even though it is impossible to know exactly which parts of the building are originally from L'Escalopier's mansion, it hardly matters. Maison Eymonaud is a delight in itself, with exquisitely carved panels and doors, encaustic tiles and grimacing gargoyles staring down at you from a bay window outside.

Compte de L'Escalopier's Mansion and Glasshouses, 1836

6. La Basilique du Sacré-Cœur

The Basilica of Sacré-Cœur

In July 1873, the National Assembly pronounced as public works, a Basilica proposed by the Archbishop of Paris. It was to be at the summit of Montmartre, financed from the public purse, and built, "to the honour of the Sacred Heart of Jesus Christ, to look upon France and to afford divine protection". Thus the 'National Vow' of 1870 for the deliverance of the Pope and the salvation of France was fulfilled. Pope Pius IX had decreed the feast day of the Sacred Heart in 1856, at the behest of the Society of Jesus. The first stone of this colossal structure was laid in 1875, on the site of the Artillery Parade and its construction painstakingly executed until its eventual consecration on 16th October 1919.

A deep division had opened up within French society. The French Revolution and later the Commune, led to the bitterly opposed factions of Church, State and Monarchy on one side, and radicals and socialists on the other. To heal wounds after the trauma of the Commune, the National Assembly felt that a symbol of unity was needed to mark an end to enmity and the beginning of a new order. The Catholic Church wanted to thank God for the deliverance of France, and to 'expiate the sins' of those who had put the nation in such great peril. From these desires sprang the Basilica of Sacré-Cœur.

Not all Parisians supported the project, feeling no need whatsoever to do penance. Worship of the Sacred Heart of Jesus was controversial in itself, due to its association with the old monarchist order. The cult had been championed by one Marguerite-Marie Alacoque, whose visions and personal entreaties had captured Louis XIV's imagination, although he was unable to fulfill his prison cell pledge to build a chapel in its

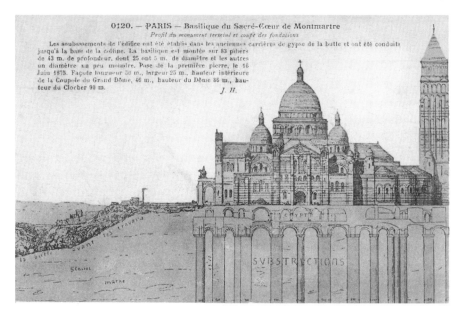

0120. — PARIS — Basilique du Sacré-Cœur de Montmartre
Profil du monument terminé et coupé des fondations
Les soubassements de l'édifice ont été établis dans les anciennes carrières de gypse de la butte et ont été conduits jusqu'à la base de la colline. La basilique est montée sur 83 piliers de 43 m. de profondeur, dont 25 ont 5 m. de diamètre et les autres un diamètre un peu moindre. Pose de la première pierre, le 16 Juin 1875. Façade longueur 50 m., largeur 25 m., hauteur intérieure de la Coupole du Grand Dôme, 46 m., hauteur du Dôme 86 m., hauteur du Clocher 90 m.
J. H.

Section showing the deep concrete piles on which the Basilica sits

honour. Marie Antoinette's final prayers as she faced the guillotine were offered up to the Sacred Heart of Jesus. The link between the cult, the monarchy and the old regime, along with its position on the very site of the Communard Artillery Parade, made the building of Sacré-Cœur hugely contentious. Eventually, the National Assembly had to declare the building a public utility and forcibly purchase the land. The issue rankled with the local population.

A national competition was held to decide on the design, which was won by the architect Paul Abadie. Unfortunately, his vast structure could not be supported where it was to stand, due to the honeycomb of disused Plaster of Paris quarries beneath the hill. The Basilica had to be underpinned with eighty-three concrete-filled piles, sunk 120 feet into the ground, a brilliant and complex feat of engineering, which took so long that Abadie died before the foundations were finished and he never saw his building completed. The final result still divides opinion.

Whether one appreciates Abadie's extravagant vision or not, the statistics are impressive. Costing an estimated 45 million francs, the Basilica was paid for partly by public subscription – you can see named and sponsored bricks inside as you walk around. Ten million donors contributed. The interior of Sacré-Cœur houses one of the largest mosaics in the world, entitled *Christ in Majesty*. At 275 feet high the bell tower holds the largest bell in France, weighing in excess of nineteen tons. Named *Le Savoyarde*, it needed eighty horses to pull it up the hill to where it was finally to sound out across the city.

7. La Colline au Néolithique

The Neolithic Mount

Thanks to its prominence, the hill of Montmartre has, since the Quaternary era, enjoyed a privileged location. The fossilised remains of its great mammals were first analysed by Cuvier in 1789. Springs and rich deposits of gypsum in the subsoil helped to support the beginnings of an early yet advanced civilisation. A simple shelter undoubtedly dates from before the arrival of the druids. Built and inhabited by the Gallic-Romans, the site displays to the west of the mount, an altar dedicated to Mercury, as well as a sanctuary honouring Mars, to the south of St Pierre's Church. From here comes the doubt over its etymology; Hilduin cites 'Mons Mercurii' in 840, and 'Mons Martis" is referred to in Abdon's 'The Siege of Paris' in 885. In the middle of the XIII century, 'The Golden Legend' by Jacques de Voragine, a text devoured by all levels of society, spread throughout Christendom the name of Mont des Martyrs – Martyrs' Mount, recounting the suffering of St Denis and his companions. Thus they eclipsed the two gods of commerce and war, apart from the period between November 1793 and December 1794, when the hill was renamed "Mont-Marat" in homage to "the friend of the people".

The origin of the name 'Montmartre' causes much debate, but there is no doubt that, like so many sites in Paris, the hill has changed its name with the times. The plaque presents a number of conflicting sources for the origin of the name. Bishop Hilduin's 840 version comes from his account of the life of Dionysus – or St Denis as he became known – in which he cites 'The Mount of Mercury' as the place of his execution. A few years later, in 885-6, Abdon, or Abbo, a Neustrian Benedictine monk, wrote a gripping eyewitness account of the Viking Siege of Paris in Latin verse, entitled *Bella Parisiacae Urbis* (The Wars of the City of Paris). He cites 'The Mount of Mars' as the name of the famous hill. His epic poem describes the ferocious battle between the Frankish defenders and Viking invaders. Their defensive strategies included pouring hot wax and pitch upon the heads of Norsemen trying to destroy the towers on the island in the Seine that constituted Paris at that time. The Seine was impassable beyond the island, so the Vikings set light to a ship and set

LE GRAND PALÉOTHÉRION.

it drifting towards the wooden bridge which connected the island to the mainland. They succeeded in burning it down, and gained passage. Just twelve men remained to defend the island fortress, all of whom refused to surrender. They were slaughtered and the Vikings sailed on to plunder Le Mans and Chartres.

Voragine's medieval blockbuster *The Golden Legend* was one of the first books to be translated into English by William Caxton and named the hill as 'The Martyrs' Mount'. Voragine's book was full of stories of

bloodshed, miracles, and various tortures visited upon the saints (10). It was hugely popular in the Middle Ages, spreading the tale of St Denis and the Christian Martyrs across Europe.

The final name change occurred after the Revolution of 1789. Several towns chose to rename themselves in memory of revolutionary leader Jean-Paul Marat after his assassination by Charlotte Corday. Montmartre was renamed 'Mont Marat' from 25th November 1789, in honour of the man who had hidden in its quarry caves.

Another reference on the plaque is to an important archaeological discovery. Near to this site, around the rue Ronsard area, miners dug up fossilised remains that they believed to be human. They sent them to the brilliant zoologist Georges Cuvier who identified the fossilised tooth of a long extinct breed of browsing equine, not unlike a modern-day tapir. Cuvier was said to be able to draw accurate pictures of prehistoric beasts from a single fossil, and in this case his skill was to prove uncannily accurate. Later excavations revealed the animal's whole skeleton, exactly as Cuvier had drawn it.

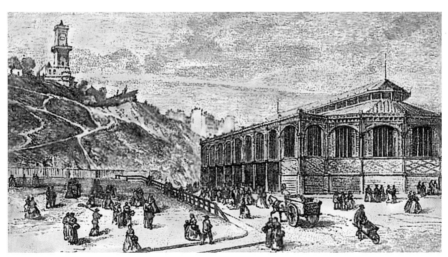

Le Marché St Pierre in 1868

8. La Folie Sandrin

Sandrin's Folly

In 1774, a M. Sandrin purchased one and a half acres of land in the heart of Montmartre village to build a luxurious country house or 'folly'. In 1795 the house was sold to a wine merchant, and then converted into a clinic in 1806 by Dr Prost, a specialist in mental illnesses and a student of Pinel. Breaking away from the tradition of keeping patients chained up in asylums, Dr Prost experimented with innovative treatments believing that, "The treatment of the mind is sometimes more efficient than conventional treatment. One should be gently compassionate as it never fails to inspire and establish trust in the patients leading them effortlessly to do what suits their state of mind". Success was not long in coming, especially from amongst the exhausted or depressed writers and artists needing attention. In 1820 Dr Esprit Blanche took over the already well-known clinic, and with his wife, who was equally inspired by the same philanthropic sentiments, Blanche strove to provide a quiet family life for his patients. From 1841 the most famous patient was Gérard de Nerval, who said, "For me, here started what I would call the realisation of a dream in real life".

The original owner of this house was Antoine Gabriel Sandrin, a teacher and candle-maker. After its sale in 1795, the beautiful country home he built here would be used as a school and, later, a military billet. But now it is primarily as a symbol of the humane treatment of psychiatric patients that it is remembered.

An inventory of the buildings in the late part of the eighteenth century tells us of a house which consisted of, "...a ground floor with cellars, topped by two floors and a large square loft with a beautiful staircase." On the ground floor was a large living room, a dining room, billiards room, pantry and kitchen, as well as stables and outhouses. There were twenty four rooms in total. Outside was a six acre garden planted with elms and further grounds with picturesque groves, rockeries and streams. These were the idyllic surroundings that Dr Prost chose for his sanatorium in 1806.

Today we abhor the notion of chaining up the mentally ill. However, prior to the emergence of psychotherapy and the invention of psychotropic drugs at the end of the nineteenth century, psychiatric medicine was still in its infancy, with only hydrotherapy, leeches, castor oil and bloodletting available as

Sandrin's Folly, 1830

the 'conventional' treatments that Prost mentions in the plaque. The famous psychiatrist Dr Pinel had begun the move towards unchaining patients in 1793 at the Bicêtre Hospital. Dr Prost, and later Dr Blanche, continued to develop his gentler model of treatment. Hydrotherapy was retained under the regimes of both doctors, which involved either alternately hot and cold baths, or swaddling and steaming patients.

Despite these archaic treatments, the improvement in the overall conditions was immeasurable. The clinic's real advances were in the compassionate attitude it fostered towards patients, with an emphasis on peace and tranquillity, combined with gentle understanding and encouragement. Under Blanche's regime, patients were encouraged to take walks around the grounds as part of their daily routine, and a small Chinese Pavilion was installed there for their use. They also shared meals and family life with Dr Blanche, so that they felt accepted and safe when their illness manifested in its sometimes frightening extremes.

Contemporary accounts describe Dr Blanche as man 'who knew how to love and how to be obeyed', and these attributes of kindness, combined with firm care, endeared Blanche to many of his patients. They would often return to drink tea with him and his family in the gardens.

Blanche was particularly welcoming to the impoverished artists who lived on the Butte, writing later about the link between madness and creativity. The romantic poet Gérard de Nerval spent many months here, and remembered the asylum fondly in his writing. Nerval owned a pet lobster called Thibault, whom he rescued from a lobster pot whilst on holiday in La Rochelle. He would take his pet for afternoon strolls in the Palais Royal gardens, on the end of a blue silk ribbon, telling his friends, "I have a liking for lobsters. They are peaceful, serious creatures. They know the secrets of the sea, they don't bark and they don't gnaw upon one's monadic privacy like dogs do..."

Although he was sometimes gravely ill, Nerval was a major poet who influenced Victor Hugo, Marcel Proust and T S Eliot. He and other artists, along with their friends, formed an impressive list of names associated with the hospital. Guy de Maupassant and Theo Van Gogh, brother of Vincent, found peace here for a while, and visitors included Renoir, Degas, Manet, Delacroix, Dumas, Satie, Gautier and Berlioz.

Dr Blanche moved his clinic in 1852 and handed its running over to his son Émile.

Dr Esprit Blanche

9. La Fusillade du 18 Mars 1871

The Shooting of 18th March 1871

After a failed night-time attempt to capture the cannons of the National Guard, the first blood was spilt on the evening of 18th March 1871. General Clément-Thomas, a veteran Republican exiled under the Empire, who had returned after the battle of Sedan to assist in the defence of Paris, was recognised in Pigalle, despite his denials and civilian attire. He was looking for General Lecomte, who had been detained that morning by insurgents for ordering his troops to shoot into the crowd. Also arrested, Clément-Thomas was taken to the headquarters of the Central Committee at No 6 rue des Rosiers (re-named in 1907 rue du Chevalier de La Barre). Summarily condemned to death, both Generals were executed against a garden wall by their own troops

There was the sound of near-riot in the streets of Pigalle. Whether by dint of soldierly duty or with reckless disregard for his own safety, General Clément-Thomas ventured out to investigate the cause of the commotion. He found a huge crowd filling the streets, haranguing a prisoner whom the National Guard were desperately trying to protect. Clément-Thomas recognised the man immediately. It was General Lecomte who was being dragged off to the Communard Headquarters at 6, rue des Rosiers - now 36 rue du Chevalier de la Barre. Lecomte had been arrested that morning for ordering his troops to fire into the crowd as he tried to seize the people's cannons **(27)**. With a mood of riot and insurrection hanging heavily in the air, Clément-Thomas made his second mistake of the day: inflaming the mob further, he shouted at them that Lecomte had "...only been following orders..." It was an error of judgement which had terrible consequences. He was recognised as the despised General

General Clément-Thomas

thought to be responsible for a massacre of insurgents in 1848. He too was seized and taken to join General Lecomte.

The escorting guards struggled to ensure the prisoners' safety as the crowds surged around them, hurling insults and abuse. It took them several hours to reach their destination. By the time they arrived, the two elderly Generals were at the mercy of a blood-thirsty rabble,

General Lecomte

who were clamouring for their execution. Captain Simon Mayer, the Commander responsible for their safety, ran to warn Dr Clemenceau of the danger. He felt that only someone of Clemenceau's stature could possibly impose himself on events, which were beginning to spiral out of control. Clemenceau immediately set off for rue de Rosiers, feeling he had disastrously miscalculated the ferocity of the mood in the city. Meanwhile, in the absence of any senior commander, the pressure of the crowd had intensified. What followed remained a stain on the conscience of the Communards. Despite the guards' repeated pleas to wait for the Committee to convene a court-martial, the crowd refused. Lecomte was shut in a ground floor room for his protection, but Clément-Thomas, arriving slightly later, was immediately bundled into the garden and stood against the wall. He was shot at, but shouted defiantly, "Kill me! You won't stop me calling you cowards and assassins!" It was not a clean execution. He finally fell dead with a gunshot through the eye. The windows of Lecomte's sanctuary were then broken and he was dragged out, to be despatched with a shot in the back.

The scene degenerated further thereafter. The bodies were desecrated by men, women and children, seemingly in the grip of mass hysteria, described later by Clemenceau as 'a savage fury...of blood lust'. By the time he arrived, shouting "Pas de sang, mes amis!" ("No blood, my friends!") it was too late. He was said to have wept when he saw what had befallen the two Generals, and the crowd revelling in their deaths. By then, however, the tide of revolution was sweeping across Paris and could not be turned. The Government withdrew to Versailles and the Commune was finally in charge of the city.

Photomontage representation the shooting

10. La Légende de Saint Denis

The Legend of Saint Denis

From the Merovingian period comes the legend of the conversion of Paris by its first bishop and missionary, sent by Pope Clement. A martyr for his faith, St Denis would die beheaded in 273, together with the priest Rustique and Archdeacon Éleuthère, only a few leagues from the city. In 475, his memory was honoured in this place when St Geneviève persuaded the people to build a basilica upon his tomb where miracles would abound. The blind and the paralysed were cured, and the devil exorcised from the possessed. In 840, Abbot Hilduin relates the remarkable legend: the saint, executed yet not ceasing to preach, picked up his head and carried it to the fountain.

St Denis is a *cephalophore*, or head-carrying saint, invoked against diabolical possession and, ironically, headaches. Little is known about Denis' formative years in Italy, but his deep piety and religious scholarship were observed at an early age. Clearly destined to be a notable missionary, he was chosen by Pope Clement to travel to Roman Paris in order to defend and spread the faith. He wasted no time in settling on the Île de la Cité and establishing a successful church, accompanied by his two close friends, Eleutherius and Rusticus. In fact, so great was his conversion rate that the enraged local pagan priests ordered his arrest.

The Archbishop of Genoa, Jacobus de Voraigne, tells the rest of the story in the *The Golden Legend* (1275), the earliest source of the tale:

"And the saints were beaten cruelly of twelve knights, and were straightly bounden with chains of iron, and put in prison. The day following, Denis was laid upon a gridiron, and stretched all naked upon the coals of fire, and there he sang to our Lord saying: Lord thy word is vehemently fiery, and thy servant is embraced in the love thereof. And after that he was put among cruel beasts, which were excited by great hunger and famine by long fasting, and as soon as they came running upon him he made the sign of the cross against them, and anon they were made most meek and tame. And after that he was cast into a furnace of fire, and the fire anon quenched, and he had neither pain ne harm. And after that he was put on the cross, and thereon he was long tormented, and after, he was taken down and put into a dark prison with his fellows and many other Christian men."

Despite the best efforts of the pagan priests, Denis refused to renounce his faith and was condemned to be executed in front of the Temple of Mercury at the top of the hill, close to where the church of St Pierre de Montmartre now stands **(37)**. The legend recounts that the Roman soldiers escorting him were too lazy to walk all the way up to the top of the hill for the main event, and decided instead to behead him half way up, where the Martyrium now stands **(36)**. In an impressive act of defiance:

".St. Denis raised himself up, and bare his head between his arms, as the angel led him two leagues from the place, which is said the hill of the martyrs, unto the place where he now resteth, preaching all the while. And there was heard so great and sweet a melody of angels that many of them that heard it believed in our Lord."

It is said he stopped to wash his head in a fountain here, in Parc Susanne Boisson, before proceeding on his way, finally collapsing in a cornfield in an area to the north of Montmartre, known now as St-Denis. First a tiny chapel, then an abbey and finally a beautiful Cathedral Basilica were built where Denis fell. The site became a place of pilgrimage and the chosen resting place for every French King but three, from Clovis in 511 to Louis XVIII in 1824.

You can see a statue of the brave saint in the park, pointing his head towards the *boules* matches being played beneath him.

St Denis, attended by angels, Notre Dame Cathedral

11. La Maison Rose de Rosimond

The House of Rose de Rosimond

Born in 1645, Claude de la Rose, alias de Rosimond, a writer when it took his fancy, was chosen to succeed Molière as the leader of the King's company of actors. Like Molière, he died on stage, at the end of performing 'The Hypochondriac'. From 1680, de Rosimond owned a country home here, surrounded by five plots of arable land and, during the 19th century, the house was converted into studios for artists. Auguste Renoir, seeking more space, rented two rooms and the old stable here. After him arrived Léon Bloy, Raoul Dufy, Suzanne Valadon, André Utter and Maurice Utrillo, amongst others. Dilapidated and threatened with demolition 1952, the oldest house of the Butte was saved by the Society of History and Archaeology (a society known as Le Vieux Montmartre), and turned into a museum in 1961.

Rosimond was the stage name of Claude de la Rose (1645-1675), a leading light in the touring theatre troupes based in and around Rouen in the mid-seventeenth century. He was talented enough to be chosen by Molière's friends and colleagues to take on the great man's acting parts after his death. Following Rosimond's own ironic final curtain, the house he bought here in rue Cortot staged a different kind of drama – that of the lives of its occupants.

Some of Montmartre's most famous painters worked from studios in this ancient building. Renoir rented a studio, or *atelier*, on the first floor in 1876, and stored his canvas *Bal au Moulin de la Galette* in one of the garden outhouses. In 1896, Suzanne Valadon rented rooms.

Marie-Clémentine, or 'Suzanne' as Toulouse-Lautrec later renamed her, was born in Bessines-sur Gartempe, Haute-Vienne, to a poor seamstress, Madeleine Valadon. Suzanne

Suzanne Valadon

Valadon went on to become one of Montmartre's most colourful and celebrated characters. She grew up running wild in the streets, drawing in chalk on the pavements. An untamable girl, she constantly played truant, preferring her freedom during the lawless days of the Commune. Her mother was taciturn and

The House of Rose de Rosimond

undemonstrative, withdrawing further and further from life. At fifteen Suzanne joined a circus but, after being injured in a fall, she worked instead as an artist's model.

At sixteen Suzanne was an artist's dream. She was captivating, with a fiery temperament, a hauntingly beautiful face and fine voluptuous curves. It wasn't long before she was modelling regularly for Puvis de Chavannes, Toulouse-Lautrec and Auguste Renoir. She loved the work, never complaining about the long hours and low pay.

By the age of eighteen Suzanne was pregnant and, on Christmas Day 1883, gave birth to a boy, who was to become the world-renowned artist Maurice Utrillo **(12)**. She always refused to confirm the identity of Maurice's father, keeping everyone guessing, and allowing the Spanish artist Miguel Utrillo to give the child his name.

It was Lautrec who spotted Suzanne's artistic talent and introduced her to Degas, who complimented the "bold and supple lines" of her work. Valadon portrayed women as strong and active, in contrast to the prevailing male presentation of the female as essentially passive. She eventually made enough money from modelling and painting for her mother to give up work and care for Maurice full time, whilst she carried on with her career unhindered. In 1894 she became the first woman painter admitted to the Société Nationale des Beaux-Arts.

After one divorce, Suzanne married André Utter, one of Maurice's friends, who was twenty-one years her junior. They moved back into the house in rue Cortot, with Maurice and Madeleine. Suzanne was plagued with anxiety about her mentally fragile son. She missed him terribly when he finally married and moved away. Looking after him had been a driving force all her life, and without him she felt lost. She died peacefully in her studios in avenue Junot in 1938.

Take some time to visit the charming, peaceful Museum of Montmartre, which is now housed here. You can find the original sign from Le Lapin Agile, zinc cut-outs from the shadow plays at Le Chat Noir, and posters by Toulouse-Lautrec.

12. La Maison Rose de Maurice Utrillo

The Pink House of Maurice Utrillo

Maurice Utrillo was born in rue du Poteau in 1883, the son of Suzanne Valadon (1867-1938), an acrobat and model encouraged by Degas, Toulouse-Lautrec and Renoir to develop her formidable expressionist talent. After his first internment in the hospital of Sainte-Anne from 1900, on the advice of his doctors his mother introduced him to painting. As attached to urban scenes as Valadon was devoted to portraiture, Utrillo broke away from traditional landscape techniques to create poetical city panoramas infused with an iridescent melancholy. Driven by a desire for perfection and the near-realism of the naïve school, most of his work portrays the streets of Montmartre. Despite his legendary status as a failed artist, he knew success from 1919. In 1955, he was buried in the Saint-Vincent cemetery, between his mother and his companion, Lucie Valore.

Maurice Utrillo, son of the artist Suzanne Valadon (11), was a disturbed and anxious child, prone to furious tempers followed by fits of weeping. As he grew up, he was often left in the care of his bad-tempered alcoholic grandmother, Madeleine, while his headstrong mother continued modelling and partying. He missed her terribly and by the age of ten began returning home from school drunk, sometimes smashing crockery and ripping up the curtains in the house.

Maurice's distress was intense, and his deep attachment to his mother made their relationship particularly fraught. His drinking worsened and at the age of eighteen he spent three months in Sainte-Anne's, a psychiatric hospital. At her wit's end, and at the suggestion of his physician Dr Ettinger, Suzanne introduced Maurice to painting. It seemed to

Suzanne with Maurice, aged 7

calm his mind, and he found a measure of peace at his easel. His early works showed

Utrillo's Pink House, circa 1890

little promise but gradually his technique improved and he developed his own unique style. His paintings seemed always to reflect the loneliness he felt. The streets of Montmartre he depicted were often empty of people, its houses shuttered and unwelcoming. One of his most popular works is a painting of the pink painted house at the end of rue Cortot, which he completed in 1912.

Utrillo remained a troubled character, often to be found in a stupor at the cabaret, Le Lapin Agile **(22)**, where he drank with Modigliani and André Utter. Despite being considered somewhat uncritical of his own work, his popularity never waned and he was made a member of the Legion of Honour in 1928. His patchy output was due, no doubt, to his ongoing illness, which continued to haunt him, and sometimes threatened to overwhelm him entirely. There were several more hospitalisations throughout his life.

In 1935, he married a rich widow, Lucie Powels Valore, and moved to Le Vésinet, not far from Paris, where he continued to paint, under his wife's firm regime. She took over his care completely, allowing him small quantities of watered-down wine. She also managed his business affairs with great skill, stopping the supply of his canvasses to the market, which increased their value immediately.

Suzanne Valadon bitterly resented Lucie and was jealous of the influence she exerted over her beloved Maurice. He seemed happy enough, however, despite the odd flash of rebellion. He became deeply religious as he grew older and Lucie took him to his favourite chapel to pray every day. He carried a gilded statue of Joan of Arc with him wherever he went.

When his mother died of a brain haemorrhage in her Paris studio in 1938, Maurice collapsed. Their bond was so great that he could not bear to attend the funeral and locked himself away for a whole year.

He slowly recovered, and continued to paint Montmartre from memory and from postcards and, despite his severe alcoholism and many years of mental ill-health, he lived to the age of seventy-four.

13. La Mire du Nord

The Point of the North

From 1670 the Academy of Sciences undertook the measuring of the longitudinal position of Paris, expressed in toises and degrees, on a meridian from Dunkirk to Barcelona. Abbot Jean Picard, director of works between Paris and Amiens, fixed a wooden pillar here on 14th August 1675, named the "Meridional Beacon". Taken up by the Cassinis, this work formed the blueprint for the map of France, and the beacon was later replaced by a stone pyramid, three metres high, and crowned with a three-petalled iris, stylized as the fleur-de-lys. The inscription reads, "In the year 1736, this obelisk was erected by order of the King, to show the alignment of Paris with the northern coast. Its axis is at 2,931 toises and two feet from the meridional face of the Observatory."

Take your atlas and draw a line through France, from Dunkirk on the channel coast to Perpignan, near the Spanish border. There you have the original Paris Meridian established in 1667 as zero degrees longitude. Later Greenwich would oust Paris as the prime meridian but the obelisk described here was built to mark the northern bearing and it still stands in the gardens of the Moulin de la Galette. It was originally planned to be one of ninety-six such markers placed along the line, from the extreme North right up to the Pyrenees. But the project never really got underway, and soon the Mire du Nord was all but abandoned, eventually becoming enclosed in the gardens of the Mill in the late 1830s.

However, herein lay a problem, since the opportunistic owner of the property refused to allow council inspectors access to it for three years. He demanded compensation to the tune of fifty-thousand francs for the inconvenience caused by the monument on his land. At various times observations had been made about the monument's state of repair. It was noted by the historian Chéronnet, in 1840, that the original pinnacle ornament – a globe – was missing from the obelisk. It had been replaced by *the fleur-de-lys* mentioned in the plaque, but by the time Chéronnet saw it, the monument was crowned with just a lance and was in a sorry condition.

Other mysteries surround the Mire du Nord. Two handwritten inscriptions intended for the base of the monument were discovered in the Paris Observatory library. They were both written anonymously in red crayon, and dated 1737. One was the couplet : *Chef-d'œuvre de l'économie /A l'honneur de l'Académie,* (Masterpiece of economy / In honour of the Academy). The meaning of the other transcription is incomprensibly obscure, and lost in time.

Much excitement was generated by the unearthing of an old stone tablet near the base, with so many letters obscured that it was all but illegible. Historians argued for some time about what the mysterious words could possibly be. There was embarrassment when it was eventually translated as a signpost saying 'Donkey Path This Way', which a quarrying team had left it behind many years before.

The 'toises' mentioned in the plaque are a unit of measure for length which originated in pre-revolutionary France, equal to roughly 1.949 metres, or six feet. The Cassinis were Jean-Dominique Cassini (1625-1712) and Jacques Cassini (1677-1756), the father and son team that carried on Picard's groundbreaking work.

If you look closely at the ground as you wander through Paris you may see, set in the asphalt, brass medallions of about 12 cm in diameter, inscribed 'Aragó N S', for North and South. These plaques commemorate the Director of the National Observatory, François Aragó (1786-1853) who successfully recalculated the Paris Meridian in the early 1800's. The medallions stretch almost six miles along the line of the Meridian, from Porte Montmartre to Cité Universitaire. The work, known as the 'invisible monument', was created by Dutch conceptual artist Jan Dibbets and the medallions number around 135.

The author Dan Brown strained creative licence when he included the Aragó medallions in a sequence from his blockbuster *The Da Vinci Code*. According to Brown, the medallions led to the grave of Mary Magdalene. Souvenir hunters have stolen several of the discs, but most remain. Keep looking down and you may just spot one.

The Mire du Nord monument

14. La Statue du Chevalier de la Barre

The Statue of the Knight of the Barre

"While the Knight of the Barre was convicted not only of singing profane songs, but also of failing to doff his hat to a procession of Capuchin monks, the judges of Abbeville ordered that, as well as having his tongue torn out, his hand cut off, and his body burned after decapitation, he first be tortured until he had confessed to how many songs he had actually sung, and to how many processions he had shown similar disrespect." Voltaire expressed his outrage in the 'Philosophical Dictionary' of 1769 at the fate of this 19-year-old, who was executed in 1766. The Republicans raised a statue to him in 1885, in the square of the Basilica Sacré-Cœur, which was moved here at the time of the opening of the public garden in 1927. It was melted down for cast iron in 1941.

Late one night in August 1765, a wooden crucifix on the bridge at Abbeville was torn down. On discovering this, the enraged Bishop of Amiens threatened to excommunicate anyone who refused to disclose information about the perpetrator of the crime. He was met with silence. Tension mounted but still no one came forward. Finally, the local magistrate, Du Maisniel de Belleval, who harboured a grudge against a young nobleman called Jean-François de la Barre, had him arrested on trumped up charges. Jean-François was also accused of disrespecting monks, singing lewd songs and owning seditious literature, including Voltaire's first *Philosophical Dictionary*, published in 1764.

The Dictionary contained alphabetically arranged articles in which Voltaire disparaged the Catholic Church and other institutions. Possession of this volume sealed the boy's fate. After chopping off his hands and removing his tongue, Jean-François was decapitated and his body thrown on a pyre in the square at Abbeville, along with a copy of the Dictionary.

Jean-François Lefebvre de la Barre (1745–1766) was a victim of that age's savage religious intolerance and remains a symbol for those committed to free speech. His case was championed by Voltaire who wrote two accounts of the case - *Relation de la Mort du Chevalier de la Barre* (1766) and *Le Cri du Sang Innocent* (1775), in which he attacks the complicity of the Catholic Church in what was in fact a prosecution raised by the State. A number of offences against religion, such as sacrilege and blasphemy, survived from the edicts of the Old Regime. De la Barre was eventually pardoned in 1794 by the National Convention.

Pictured is the original statue, before it was melted down by the Vichy government for the Nazi war effort. The stone base remained and a new statue of Jean-François de la Barre, by sculptor Emmanuel Ball, was erected on 24th February 2001 in a ceremony that celebrated humanism and free speech.

The original statue outside Sacré-Cœur

15. Le Bal du Château Rouge

The Ballroom of The Château Rouge

At the end of the 18th century a great brick pavilion was built here, one storey high, with carved corner stones, crowned with a high loft. Its name no doubt comes from the colour of the materials employed. In 1844, a major clearance sacrificed trees and bushes for the opening of the streets Poulet, Custine, Myrrha, and Château-Rouge (later Clignancourt). A M. Boboeuf acquired the pavilion in 1845 to launch the "New Tivoli, Ballroom of the Château-Rouge". Success soon followed, and the place was selected in July 1847 to hold the first of the Reformist banquets, as preludes to the 1848 Revolution. After a period of glory under the 2nd Empire, it began its decline, and the building was sold in 1881.

Once it was a fine mansion of red brick but today Château Rouge is no more than a stop on the métro. In 1787, the building was described as 'a charming house whose gardens measure about thirty acres' and, no doubt due to the architectural similarity it bore to the Place des Vosges, a legend persisted that it once housed Henry IV's beautiful blonde mistress Gabrielle d'Estrées. Its original owner was in fact Squire Christophe. The poor Squire nearly lost his house during the Revolution of 1789, when M.

Fournier, commander of the local constabulary, whipped up a mob to search the Château for grain. Seen as a possible 'monopolist' hiding grain in order to hike prices and keep people starving, Christophe saw his property ransacked. The mob found nothing and he was allowed to stay.

The Château's next dramatic role was in 1814, when Napoleon Bonaparte's brother, Joseph, set up his headquarters there to lead the defence of Paris against the Russian and Prussian armies. The defeated Napoleon had fled to Fontainebleau. Joseph stayed just long enough to spy the advancing troops through a telescope from an upstairs window before he too abandoned Paris for Blois, leaving Marshal Moncey to make the last stand in place de Clichy (36).

In 1843, the Château was owned by one Madame Ozanne, who specialised in second-hand bejewelled ball-gowns, which could be pawned when their owners hit hard times. Such traders often made a very good living running prostitutes as a sideline. She died leaving the Château derelict however, overrun by her beloved stray cats, its walls cracked and peeling, and the grounds ruined. Her heirs sold the land to property developers and the Château to a Monsieur Boboeuf. The developers cleared the parkland and built new roads. Monsieur Boboeuf created the most famous ballroom in Paris.

Château Rouge became the home of new Polish and Hungarian dances, such as the Polka and the Mazurka, which revolutionised ideas about what was acceptable in public between the sexes. Couples danced together instead of

Republic. In the build up, the Republicans hit upon the idea of 'Reformist Banquets' to circumvent the strict laws which banned public meetings. Château Rouge was the perfect venue. Guests paid to eat and listen to anti-monarchist speeches, sitting around long tables set up in tents outside, with musicians playing over the murmur of political debate. Later, at the height of the Revolution, troops were garrisoned in the Château. But Boboeuf was never compensated for this invasion and he was declared bankrupt in 1849. His successor ran a

Dancing the quadrille – a rare image by Don Jean from sheet music

in lines. Heaven forbid! Boboeuf also installed coloured gas lanterns in the park outside, creating a magical garden, glittering with lights. He allowed entertainers to delight his guests as they wandered in the grounds between dances.

Boboeuf also rented his premises out for private functions, and it was in this capacity that the Château next made the history books. The 'February Revolution' of 1848 saw Republicans take up arms against the unpopular Charles X, and install Bonaparte's nephew Napoleon III as the head of the Second

less respectable ball, and the Can-Can police were deployed to ensure that new dance crazes did not outrage public morals.

In 1870, during the Siege, the Château was again used as a barracks and throughout the Commune it was the Communard Headquarters. It was here that General Lecomte was taken before his date with a firing squad **(9)**. Soon after the Commune, the Château was sold and demolished. Nothing of it remains.

16. Le Bateau-Lavoir

The Laundry Boat

"We shall all go back to the Bateau-Lavoir. Only there, were we truly happy..." Until his death, Picasso (1881-1973) remained nostalgic for the rural Montmartre he knew during his youth, with its farms, its orchards and its picturesque cabarets. Arriving on the Butte at the age of 19, he took a studio here in 1904 where he painted his last works from the Blue Period, and those from the Pink Period, inspired by his affair with Fernande Olivier, as well as the 'Demoiselles d'Avignon' (1907), the prelude to Cubism. Better known as the 'Maison du Trappeur' (The Trapper's House), the former piano factory was divided into studios around 1889 and renamed by Max Jacob. A fire on 12th May 1970 reduced its large wooden sheds and maze of passageways and stairs to ashes.

It is hard to grasp the historical and cultural significance of the buildings that stood at No. 13 place Émile Goudeau. Yet it was here, in a row of dilapidated, ramshackle studios that Paris saw the birth of Cubism - the next great artistic movement to follow Impressionism. Max Jacob's nickname for the buildings stemmed from their visual similarity to the laundry boats that worked on the Seine. Apparently the floorboards also creaked like the wooden planks of a ship.

In 1904 an unknown Spanish artist called Pablo Ruiz Picasso moved into the Bateau-Lavoir. Fernande Olivier, the lover whom he first met in a rainstorm in the square outside, describes the atmosphere in her memoirs,

"...a weird, squalid building echoing from morning to night with every kind of noise: discussion, singing, shouting, calling, the sound of buckets used to empty the toilet clattering noisily on the floor ... doors slammed, suggestive moaning coming through the closed doors..."

Picasso, 1904

There was only one tap in the entire building, and conditions were hopelessly cramped. Picasso and Fernande's stormy affair played out against this backdrop. Picasso, who was fiercely possessive, often locked her in his

A Laundry Boat

Le Bateau-Lavoir

rooms when he went out, preventing her from mixing with or modelling for other men.

Fernande was Picasso's muse and, as the plaque describes, inspired by her he moved out of his 'Blue' and on to his 'Pink' Period. These expressions refer to periods when he restricted his palette predominantly to these colours, reflecting his changing mood. Picasso had spent the three years in mourning for the his best friend, Carlos Casagemas, who had committed suicide in Paris when spurned by his lover, Germaine. Picasso's depression was fed by his guilt for subsequently starting an affair with the same woman. She can be seen in his painting, *At The Lapin Agile* (1905), where she stands next to Picasso, who is dressed as a harlequin. By this time he was just beginning to emerge from deep sadness, and his new love affair with Fernande Olivier lifted him further.

Amidst the squalor, famous thinkers, poets, artists and writers came and went, including Modigliani, Matisse, Gertrude Stein, Apollinaire, Juan Gris, Utrillo, Kees Van Dongen, and Brancusi. From this artistic ferment Cubism was born. Picasso, who was heavily influenced at that time by Cezanne and African art and sculpture, began to reject the idea of the artist depicting the subject from just one viewpoint. Instead he presented it from many different viewpoints in an abstract fragmented form, with all the planes overlapping and interpenetrating, which gave virtually no sense of perspective.

The first such work was *Les Demoiselles d'Avignon*, which he began to work on at the Bateau-Lavoir in 1906. Initially Picasso showed the work only to close friends, declaring himself 'afraid of it'. Not even his radical peers understood it. Some laughed, some moved out of his circle, mystified by his obsessive conviction that this was the next great artistic direction. Few, it seemed, could accept Picasso's vision, and the Butte was scandalised by his bold leap of artistic perception. However, in time this piece became known as the 'first painting of the 20th century' and Georges Braque, although initially disturbed by the painting, would eventually work very closely with Picasso on the development of Cubism.

It was perhaps inevitable that such a radical artistic concept would flourish in the intellectual milieu which encompassed Freud's revelations on the nature of the unconscious, and Einstein's on the nature of time and relativity. The nature of consciousness was being explored and the very concept of distance and space re-evaluated. Picasso's work merely extended the revolution in thinking. Modernism was born and at Le Bateau-Lavoir it took some of its very first steps.

17. Le Cat's Cottage de Steinlen

Steinlen's Cat's Cottage

"One must act: the world is not as it should be!" proclaimed Théophile-Alexandre Steinlen, dubbed by Jules Renard, "the incorruptible eye". Born in Lausanne in 1859, he came to live in Montmartre in 1878, living first in Allée des Brouillards, before settling, surrounded by his clutter of cats, in the Bavarian pavilion. Bought up after the demolition of the 1900 Exhibition, it was re-built here at the edge of the 'Maquis'. This multi-talented and prolific innovator, inspired by a committed humanism, moved effortlessly from portrait to poster, lyrical allegory to depictions of the works of Anatole France or of Jehan Rictus. Via Picasso, his influence shaped the avant-garde movement of the early 20th century. In 1923, he was laid to rest in the cemetery of St Vincent.

Steinlen's iconic street cat poster, created for Le Chat Noir (18), has become emblematic of Parisian cabaret life of the late 1800's, accurately representing its very essence as slightly wild and dangerous. It became a defining image of the Art Nouveau period, but Steinlen's legacy is much greater than this. He was primarily a social commentator and satirist, always concerned with the pitiful living conditions of the poor. A humanist and pacifist, he felt deeply about human suffering, and used Le Chat Noir magazine to express his political views with ferocious satirical humour. Steinlen was working at a time which coincided with a revolution in print – the invention of lithography in 1878. Mass production of printed material became possible. Steinlen's illustrations appeared in over fifty-five different journals and magazines, exerting a powerful influence on artists such as Toulouse-Lautrec and the young Picasso, who paid direct homage to him in their work.

But it is primarily for his sensitive drawings of cats that Steinlen is known, and his affinity for the creatures he draws is clear. It is said that the sheer number of cats he kept drove his wife to distraction. It is easy to imagine them prowling through the cottage, or hunting in the leafy Maquis opposite. He felt that only by being permanently surrounded by so many cats could he capture their essence accurately, and it is this intimate knowledge of the movement and nature of the feline that has endeared his work to so many cat lovers worldwide.

Steinlen bought the cottage (right) from the Bavarian Pavilion at the *Exposition Universelle* of 1900. Almost every nation submitted a miniature building in their own national style, and in this cottage Steinlen saw a home he wanted. He had it transported here, to the edge of the Maquis (23). It is a fairytale cottage, as charming as its name suggests, now a private residence. Beautifully maintained, it sits in a leafy green oasis behind the modern building that masks it from public view.

Steinlen's Cat's Cottage

18. Le Chat Noir

The Black Cat

Born in 1852 in Chatellerault, Rodolphe Salis created a cabaret here, where, amid a remarkable array of 'genuine Louis XIII' style furniture, he attracted the artists from the Butte and the cream of the 'Club des Hydropathes', led by the journalist Émile Goudeau. From its flamboyant launch in 1881, the tone was set, where the targets were the bourgeois clientele and their institutions. Success came quickly to this "rowdy and irreverent citadel from where the missiles fall heavily upon the gatekeepers of the boulevard as well as the mummies of the Academy", and led to the founding of a weekly magazine. In 1891 Alphonse Allais became editor of this "mouthpiece for the interests of Montmartre", led by his belief that, "…a joke is the only weapon we have against solemnity…"

The iconic 'Chat Noir', or Black Cat cabaret, will always feature in a list of Parisian institutions. But what was the cabaret of Le Chat Noir, and why was it so important in late nineteenth century Paris? The term 'cabaret' at that time was used differently from how we understand it today, and meant a tavern where the wittiest satirists, the cleverest poets and the finest musicians met to exchange ideas and routines. And of course to drink. The entertainment was often spontaneous, and raucous – a superb testing ground for new work amongst a firm but fine audience of critics.

In 1878, two years before the opening of Le Chat Noir, a group of artists and thinkers, led by the poet Émile Goudeau, formed a club they named *Les Hydropathes* ('those allergic to water'). Rodolphe Salis had been holding similar meetings in his apartment for some time, but their popularity forced him to move to larger premises. *Les Hydropathes* joined Rodolphe Salis' group in 1880, moving from their regular meeting place in a Left Bank café.

Whether intentional or not, a link between bohemianism and commerce was forged in this move. The venue became the talk of the town, with more and more artistic celebrities and – quelle horreur! – the bourgeoisie dropping by to see what all the fuss was about. But none were spared the wicked humour of the *chansonniers* at Le Chat Noir – one entered at one's own risk.

The interior of the cabaret was distinctive, decorated with heavy antique furniture and old suits of armour. A Swiss guard in full regalia greeted patrons at the door. Later Le Chat Noir shadow plays had the whole of Paris enchanted, forcing a further expansion of the club. The shows used silhouettes cut from sheets of zinc and projected via a light source onto a white silk screen. They were extremely beautiful, with dreamlike landscapes, and exquisitely fine figures. The stories and music were provided by patrons of the club. You can see some that have survived at the Museum of Montmartre in rue Cortot.

Erik Satie was the resident pianist for a while, and before long the cabaret began publishing its own magazine, full of poetry, cartoons and biting satirical observations about the bourgeoisie. Salis produced twenty thousand copies – a huge print run for the time.

Le Chat Noir's reputation was sealed as a meeting point for the greatest creative minds of that era, and it captured the mood of the new age of artistic freedom and political commentary that was such a dominant feature of Paris at that time. It closed its doors in 1897, and Salis died the same year. Debussy, Guy de Maupassant, Paul Signac, August Strindberg, Paul Verlaine, and Toulouse-Lautrec had crossed its threshold. Such was its fame that Picasso came to look for it when he arrived in Paris for the *Exposition Universelle* of 1900. He was disappointed to find that Le Chat Noir was gone.

Le Chat Noir cabaret

19. Le Château des Brouillards

Mansion of the Mists

Despite the myth, this folly constructed in 1772 was not intended for the writer Lefranc de Pompignan but for a lawyer of the Parliament of Paris. The mansion's poetic name originates no doubt from the vapours created by neighbouring water sources coming into contact with the cold air. In 1854, Gérard de Nerval dreamed of a perfect oasis of peace there: in 'L'Illustration' he wrote, "…in this small space dominated by tall trees I was first seduced by the remains of the vineyards, a remembrance of St Denis…, by the lively evening spectacle of dogs and horses at the drinking-trough… It also was an alluring place to withdraw to, silent from time to time…" In ruins and threatened with demolition, the Château des Brouillards was restored between 1922 and 1926.

In the 17th century, the area around this site was open agricultural land with a mill, farmhouse and orchards, all tumbling down the hill over to the north. Lawyer M. Legrand-Duchampjean bought the vast 7,000 square metre park and built Château des Brouillards on the remains of the farmhouse, which he used as a hunting-lodge. He sold it just before the Revolution.

In 1850, the outbuildings surrounding the Château were cleared and a number of small plots created, bounded by hedges and let at a low rent. The artists Steinlen, Poulbot and Modigliani lived there, as well as the writers Roland Dorgelès, and Leon Bloy. In 1932, Dorgelès wrote *Le Château des Brouillards*, which describes the peaceful country atmosphere of Montmartre Village.

In 1846, the poet Gérard de Nerval lived in the Château, and the quotation on the plaque is from an article called 'Walks and Memories', which he submitted to the weekly newspaper *L'Illustration* in 1854. Its tone is very much one of longing and nostalgia for the peaceful location and rural charm that Dorgelès echoed in his novel years later.

Without doubt the Château's most famous occupant was the Impressionist artist Pierre-Auguste Renoir, who lived here from 1889 and who locals say was often to be seen sitting on the front steps, peacefully smoking his pipe. He spent several artistically productive years here. The open ground surrounding the house was still a patchwork of makeshift dwellings, which merged with the Maquis **(23)**, a wasteland inhabited by determined and imaginative outsiders, attracted by the anonymity and freedom they found there.

Renoir later moved just opposite to No. 8 Allée des Brouillards, where he welcomed another artist into the world – his son, the film-maker Jean Renoir, who was born in 1894.

Jean Renoir vividly recalls the childhood he spent here with his older brother Pierre and little brother Claude, known to all as 'Coco'. He describes their daily walks across the fields to hunt for snails with his beloved nurse Gabrielle, and recalls the taste and smell of the pears in his father's orchard.

The land around the Château was full of adventure for young Jean, who remembers the eccentric poets and artists who wandered the Maquis, always on the lookout for hospitality. One regular visitor to the Château was the eccentric poet 'Bibi-la-Purée', who was famed for stealing umbrellas. He would drop in almost daily to Renoir's pantry for handouts from his wife Aline, in return for impromptu poetry recitals. He later became Verlaine's secretary and lover, his poetry lauded by Picasso, Joyce, and the whole of the Left Bank. But for a while

he was a familiar sight at Château des Brouillards in his tattered coat, coloured waistcoat and battered hat.

The brick façade which joined two buildings together was added in the 19th century, and gave a rather grand air to what was formally a run-down set of rural buildings. Divided into multiple dwellings, the house was never particularly well maintained by its landlord. But, in 1920, the entire Château was bought by Victor Perrot, local historian and President of *Le Vieux Montmartre* (The Society of Old Montmartre). Mercifully, he rescued the building from total decay. It is now divided into two private residences.

Château des Brouillards

20. Le Cimetière Montmartre

Montmartre Cemetery

During the 18th century, this land provided access to the numerous limestone quarries on the hill. Turned into a communal grave for the victims of the riots during the Revolution, it retained its role as a burial ground with rather macabre associations, under the name of 'Cemetery of the White Barricade'. Corpses, having been transferred from the capital after the closing of all inner-Parisian cemeteries for reasons of public health, were buried there in deplorable conditions. Officially opened on 1st January 1825, the North Cemetery was protected against tomb raiders and in 1856 lost one of its guardians, M. de Vaulabelle. The inventor of a system of fire-armed traps, he became a victim of his own device, taking a lethal shot in the chest!

Montmartre Cemetery was one of four cemeteries commissioned in 1786 after the closing of the Cimetière des Innocents near Les Halles. Napoleon ordered the vast over-filled burial pits to be emptied, as inadequately buried bodies were beginning to spread disease and a terrible odour across the city. In its place Montmartre Cemetery was built in the north, the vast Père Lachaise in the east, Passy Cemetery in the west and Montparnasse in the south. The terrible task of moving bodies took place over a number of months, and always under cover of darkness.

If you have an appreciation of the gothic in the shape of ancient ivy-clad gravestones then a visit to Montmartre Cemetery is the perfect way to spend an afternoon. Not as overwhelming as Père Lachaise, it has a more intimate, almost villagey feel, with boulevards in the thirty-three Divisions neatly marked by iron signposts and a map to help you navigate your way around. A stroll down the cemetery's boulevard Cité Véron is a guilty pleasure. Visually, the old graves are compelling. There is a distinct aesthetic in the peeling paint on the tumble of tombs, and colours muted by the passage of time. Amongst the iron and stone, statues of astonishing beauty appear suddenly, green with verdigris, and contrasting sharply with the surrounding decay in their almost perfect preservation of line. It is virtually impossible to take a bad photograph here.

There is life amongst the graves too: cats slide about like furry-coated spies, sizing you up as a potential food-bearer. Sometimes they simply lie asleep in the sun, poured across the warm stones. All appear affected by the gloominess of their surroundings, all a little moth-eaten and lean. Rumours of kind-hearted midnight cat feeders infuriate the present-day curators almost as much as tomb raiders did poor M. de Vaulabelle, in 1856, although thankfully they do not resort to his lethal methods of deterrent. A polite notice not to feed the cats is enough.

These morose moggies sleep in illustrious company. Montmartre Cemetery is an exclusive address and the inhabitants reflect the creative character of the area, with many artists, poets, writers and musicians who chose to make this hill their home. The graves of Offenbach and Berlioz, Degas, Dumas, Poulbot, Zola, Murger, Stendhal and Nijinsky can be found here, as well as more recent celebrities like Dalida and François Truffaut. One of Montmartre's poorest, *La Goulue*, the famous dancer of the Moulin Rouge **(26)** is here too, seemingly always with a fresh floral tribute.

Ask at the attendant's kiosk just inside the gate and they will give you a map, or you can refer to the one at the entrance, which is situated at the end of avenue Rachel, under the bridge. Be sure to isten out for the late afternoon bell warning you that the cemetery is about to close.

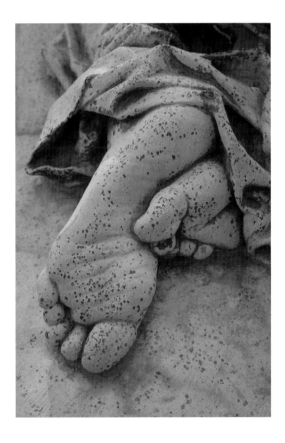

21. Le Dispensaire de Clemenceau

Clemenceau's Clinic

A physician by vocation, family tradition, and almost by public calling, Georges Clemenceau, who was born in the Vendée in 1841, completed his studies in Paris. After a visit to America, he opened a small clinic here, where despite pressing political duties, he would work until 1906. An innovator in the field of Occupational Health, he condemned the industrial uses of toxic materials, such as white lead, and would engage closely in the work of the Parisian Municipal Council, particularly through community issues and social hygiene. Elected Mayor of the 18th arrondissement on the morning of 4th September 1870, he tried in vain to dissuade General Lecomte from removing the cannons from the Butte as the day dawned on 18th March 1871.

Perhaps, upon being rejected by his people as President of the Third Republic, he pondered the maxim that all political careers end in failure. From the time of Bonaparte III, through to the defeat by Prussia, to the First World War and the rise of Nazism in neighbouring Germany, Georges Clemenceau was a towering figure in French public life.

"In order to act you must be somewhat insane. A reasonably sensible man is satisfied with thinking." And act he did, as teacher, journalist, doctor, prisoner, novelist, warrior, playwright, even duellist. But above all he was a supreme political operator, a thorn in the side of the powerful, at least when he was not in power himself. For almost sixty years the man known as Le Tigre and Père Victoire was rarely far from the momentous events that tested the nation..

Strongly influenced by his fervently republican father Benjamin, himself a village doctor, it seemed inevitable that Georges

Clemenceau, 1874

would follow in his footsteps. But, before qualifying, Clemenceau mixed with Republican hotheads in the Latin Quarter, and established a radical newspaper called *Le Travail*. In 1862 he found himself under arrest, accused of inciting political demonstrations and was imprisoned for seventy-seven days. Undeterred, he continued to be politically active after his release. The following year, due to the rising political temperature amongst Imperialists towards dissidents, he moved to New York where he wrote newspaper articles, and met his future wife, Mary Elizabeth Plummer. It was only 1869 that he returned to Paris, where he set up this clinic in Montmartre in rue des Trois Frères. He was deeply affected by the social conditions of the poor he encountered and treated the sick free of charge.

Soon afterwards Paris was plunged into the turmoil of the Siege and then the Commune. Having gained the trust and respect of the Montmartrois, Clemenceau was immediately voted Mayor of Montmartre and set about his duties with all the intelligence and energy that was to exemplify his years of public service. His political career began in earnest from this point onwards, the start of a journey that ended with

him at the centre of the world stage at the Versailles Peace Conference in 1919.

Clemenceau was an internationalist; he opposed the spread of French colonialism, admired the deep-rooted democracy of the young USA, and through the Entente Cordiale, ended centuries of antagonism with Great Britain. However, his opposition to leniency for the defeated Germany after the Great War would cultivate vast resentment. At Clemenceau's behest, the Versailles Treaty exacted harsh reparations and set the continent on course for the Second World War.

Whilst in power, Clemenceau refused to live in official residences, which he considered merely "furnished flats". He preferred his modest, rented accommodation in rue Franklin, where a museum now safeguards the possessions of the 'The Tiger', who, incidentally, never lost his bite.

Despite his astonishing career, Clemenceau ran this free clinic for thirty-seven years.

Versailles Peace Conference: Lloyd George, Signor Orlando, Clemenceau and Woodrow Wilson

22. Le Lapin Agile

The Frisky Rabbit

Around 1860, the 'Cabaret des Assassins' offered Parisians in search of the picturesque a light red wine and a welcoming terrace in the shade of a tall acacia tree. In 1886, the cabaret was converted to an inn by a former dancer and first-class cook. It played host to its regulars, amongst whom were Alphonse Allais, Caran d'Ache and André Gill, who decorated the facade with the painting of a rabbit escaping a saucepan. As a consequence, customers got used to calling the cabaret 'Lapin à Gill' [Gill's rabbit], which quickly became 'Lapin Agile' or 'Frisky Rabbit'. Bought in 1902 by Aristide Bruant, the cabaret was entrusted to the husband-and-wife managers, Berthe and Frédé, who became famous for the warm welcome they afforded impoverished painters such as Picasso, Modigliani, and Utrillo. Even the donkey, Lolo, had his hour of glory in the 1910 Salon des Indépendants, under the pseudonym of Boronali, a rather obvious anagram of Aliboron. Lolo created 'Sunset over the Adriatic' by having his tail dipped into different coloured jars of paint. Dorgelès, the inspiration of the hoax, wrote an article of futuristic fervour. "Excess in art is a strength", he wrote, "It is time to be dazzled by genius!" before revealing the truth to the press, verified by a court official.

This little building seems somewhat out of place, with its concrete faux wooden fence posts and salmon pink walls. Do not be deceived. It used to be the cabaret venue at the very centre of bohemian life in Montmartre, eventually patronised by the glitterati and immortalised in paintings. The little inn was originally named The Assassin's Cabaret because of the macabre paintings of celebrity murderers that hung on the walls, such as the regicide François Ravaillac, and the spree-killer Jean-Baptiste Troppmann. In 1902 the macabre gave way to the warmth and hospitality of Frédé and his wife Berthe. Frédé, an eccentric musician and potter who wore brightly coloured velvet waistcoats and tasselled hats, delighted in hosting joyous nights of music, poetry and song for local artists and, under his tenure, the inn became a centre for lively discussion.

However, rivalries remained between the regular clientele. Picasso's art led to the writer

Roland Dorgelès perpetrating his famous donkey-art hoax, designed to make a fool both of the Salon des Indépendants and the emerging 'new art' which he abhorred. Aliboron, or Lolo, as he was affectionately known, achieved donkey fame with his painting of a ship on the sea at sunset, created with his tail-brush. Frédé held various vegetables in front of Lolo's nose to encourage him to swish his tail with excitement. This artwork was the first of the new 'Excessivism' Movement, by a newly discovered artist called Joachim-Raphaël Boronali, wrote Dorgeles for a credulous Salon. The painting was purchased for 400 francs before the trick was revealed. Lolo became a much-loved mascot, often seen at parties with his artist friends.

Frédé often accepted paintings as payment for bar bills, amongst them Picasso's self-portrait as a harlequin, *Au Lapin Agile* (1904), in which Frédé can be seen playing his guitar in the background. Years later the painting fetched $41 million at a Sotheby's auction. Another of Picasso's painting from this time is *Femme à la Cornielle* (1904), which shows Frédé's daughter Margot cradling her tame crow.

The venue still hosts evenings of singing and poetry recitals, and the atmosphere is still intimate and engaging. The small inner room has remained virtually unchanged over the years. You can trace the history of the venue through the carvings on the ancient tables, where countless visitors have left their names. Perhaps you will be sitting where Eleanor Roosevelt sat, or Ernest Hemingway, Laurence Olivier, Vivien Leigh, Paul Newman or Henry Miller. Charlie Chaplin even played his violin here once. Many of these guests have signed and left cartoons in the visitor's book, pages from which can be seen 'virtually' on the venue's website.

Frédé and his beloved Lolo

23. Le Maquis

The Scrubland

On the southern side of rue Caulaincourt, there opened in the 19th century a warren of small twisting alleys, allotments, cabins and cottages. Goats would graze freely on these slopes. This expanse of land, named Le Maquis, was the delight of children playing truant, petty criminals, and painters drawn as much by its charm as for its cheap accommodation. Van Gogh, Steinlen, Van Dongen and Modigliani would all lodge here as they arrived in Paris. Dressed in short cloaks and tunics, Isadora Duncan and her pupils rehearsed their Greek dances barefoot in the sand, at a place ironically dubbed "the beach". Condemned in 1902 to make way for Avenue Junot, the Maquis took twenty years to disappear.

The Maquis was an area of wasteland, classed as 'unusable' by developers due to its waterlogged clay soil. Nature had gained the upper hand and the land was overgrown by a thick tangle of lilac, hawthorn and rose bushes. In the absence of any commercial interest in the plot, criminals, artists and misfits began to move in, patching together homes out of discarded building materials. The result was a shanty-town, albeit in the most peaceful area of Montmartre. Rabbits bred and goats grazed in the scrub, and a herd of cows appeared, tended by the mysterious and obsessive M.Geoffrey, who worked into the night on his vegetable plot, spied on by the young Renoir children who lived nearby. The small-scale self-sufficiency that could be achieved on the Maquis kept many from starvation. Rabbits could always be trapped and snails hunted.

Although the Maquis was a miserable piece of land, it was also free from scrutiny, which made it particularly attractive to those with something to hide. The police gave the area a wide berth, and illegal activities flourished, including money counterfeiting, illegal brewing and fraud. Left undisturbed, a gang of money-forgers managed to manufacture over fifty thousand francs and buy a Swiss castle on the proceeds! The house they had built in the

Maquis was a grand affair with a Swiss theme, a well-tended lawn and cowbells hanging in the trees surrounding the garden. Inside there was even a cuckoo clock. When they were eventually discovered they fled before the police could catch them, easily losing their pursuers in the maze of paths that ran through the Maquis. These paths were well known to inhabitants, but a baffling labyrinth to outsiders.

It is interesting to note that *Le Maquis* was also the name given to the rural wartime French Resistance, since they too hid in scrubland to avoid detection. The word 'maquis' comes from *macchia*, the Italian word for areas of gorse and scrub.

The area was finally bulldozed at the turn of the century, and the elegant avenue Junot built in its place. Avenue Junot is a treasure-trove, with architectural gems wherever you look. For lovers of Art Deco it is a treat. The artist Poulbot, who lived in the Maquis in his wilder youth, finally returned once the area had been gentrified, building the house at Number 13. High on the wall you can see the eponymous 'Poulbots', or street urchins, of Montmartre for which he became so famous. Next to Poulbot's house, at Number 15, is a modernist building of significant historical importance, designed for the famous Dadaist poet and art critic Tristan Tzara by the Austrian architect Adolf Loos.

If you peer through the railings to the right of this building you will see the only remnant of the leafy Maquis, and the mysterious *Rocher de la Sorcière* or Witch's Rock, mischievously named by local children after an elderly local eccentric.

Edith Piaf, Paul Gauguin, Modigliani and Suzanne Valadon were all residents in Avenue Junot. The contrast with the former Maquis could not be greater: the barefoot Isadora Duncan gave way to the well-heeled bohemian intelligentsia, and the transformation was complete.

The Maquis

24. Le Mariage de Verlaine

The Marriage of Verlaine

In June 1868, Paul Verlaine, the author of 'Saturnine Poems' and 'Les Fêtes Galantes', met a "pure apparition who sings and sparkles", the step-sister of his friend Charles de Sivry. The following year Verlaine proposed to the 16-year-old girl, Mathilde Mauté de Fleurville, and dedicated a collection of poems to her entitled 'The Good Song'. Victor Hugo described these works as a "flower inside an artillery shell".

> *"United by the strongest and dearest bond,*
> *Indestructible as a diamond.*
> *We will smile at everything*
> *And be afraid of nothing."*

The wedding took place on 11th August 1870. After the Commune, the young couple settled here on the second floor of their in-laws' town house. Their son Georges was born here on 30th October 1871. However, after September the seemingly unbreakable love was smashed as Verlaine fell in love with the "most handsome of wicked angels", Rimbaud. Following scandals and vain attempts at reconciliation, Verlaine was sent to a Brussels prison in 1873, after which Mathilde undertook separation procedures. "A year in paradise, a year in hell and continuous misery, these were my two years of marriage."

Verlaine and Mathilde's marriage was perhaps doomed from the beginning, and certainly justified the misgivings of Mathilde's father, who was very much against the union. Verlaine was already showing signs of alcoholism and had strong homosexual leanings when he met sixteen-year-old Mathilde. The experiment failed, and ended in misery for both of them when a young poet called Arthur Rimbaud appeared in their lives. Furious rows between Mathilde and Verlaine ensued, with the poet becoming increasingly violent towards her and his baby son, Georges.

The story of Paul Verlaine and Arthur

Rimbaud is one of scandal and excess. Two of the most gifted poets of their age, they experimented with poetry and absinthe in equal measure. Born in Charleville in 1854, Rimbaud showed early potential. At 17, he was urged to send his poetry to the then established poet Paul Verlaine, who offered to meet him. They began a passionate affair almost immediately.

Mathilde and baby Georges were abandoned as the two pursued a reckless bohemian life together. Rimbaud's bizarre and uncouth behaviour alienated most of Verlaine's friends. Known as 'Symbolist' poets of the Decadent movement, they drew on the subconscious, with emphasis on capturing extreme emotions and sensations. Both were pioneers of *vers libre* or 'free verse', the unrhymed poetry with which modern readers are now so familiar.

The lovers lived in poverty in London and the relationship began to disintegrate. They separated for a short time, but were reunited in Brussels in July 1873. However, during a furious drink-fuelled argument Verlaine fired two shots at Rimbaud, injuring his wrist. Reluctantly, Rimbaud begged the police to charge his lover with the assault, as he began to fear for his life. Verlaine's behaviour was becoming increasingly erratic. Rimbaud later withdrew his complaint, but the police still imprisoned Verlaine for two years.

Rimbaud stopped writing by the age of twenty-one, but he is a cited influence on many present-day artists, musicians and poets. He eventually went to Africa to work as a trader, and died of cancer aged just 37. Although he achieved wide recognition Paul Verlaine never found happiness and drank himself to death by the age of 52. Thousands followed his coffin to Batignolles cemetery

Above, Verlaine and Mathilde's house.
Right, Arthur Rimbaud (top) and Paul Verlaine

25. Moulin de la Galette

The Pancake Mill

More than an institution, the old 'Blute-fin' is a monument with an heroic past. In 1814, during the siege of Paris by the Cossacks, the last of four brothers of the Debray family, a dynasty of millers dating back to 1621, after a desperate defence was quartered and nailed to the sails of his windmill. After the Restoration, his sons turned the building into a dance hall, the décor consisting mainly of green-painted garden trellis. The atmosphere there was relaxed, and the customers more working-class than in other venues, as portrayed in the Renoir tableau, 'The Moulin de la Galette', painted in 1876. After a variety of incarnations, the old 'Blute-fin' was conserved in 1979.

Look high above the entrance gate to Le Moulin de la Galette on rue Lepic and you will glimpse *La Blute-fin* (literally 'The Fine Sifter', from *bluter*, to sift and *fin*, fine). This is the restored windmill that once formed the centrepiece of the Moulin de la Galette dance hall. At first it was just a modest bar serving wine and buckwheat pancakes made with the miller's own flour. But as its popularity grew so did the venue. The Debrays added electric lighting, paper lanterns and green painted trellis fencing to the dance area surrounding the windmill. On Sundays it became a respectable venue where young women were chaperoned by mothers or aunts, but on Monday evenings the clientele were altogether different.

It was a Sunday afternoon that Renoir depicted in perhaps his most famous canvas, *Bal du Moulin de la Galette* (1876), when the dance was frequented mainly by the young working-class men and women of Montmartre. He presents an idyllic scene, with friends and lovers mingling in the dappled afternoon sunlight under the acacia trees. Renoir, like many of the Impressionists, insisted on painting outdoors, *en plein air*, in order to capture the colours and light directly as he saw them. This emphasis on natural light, along with the preference for painting scenes of everyday life, were two of the main concerns of the Impressionist artists. It was when painting outside that they began to perceive that shadows were not dull and colourless, but reflected the colours of the surrounding scenery.

Renoir was using the studios at 12, rue Cortot (11) at this time, and his friends helped him carry the painting up the hill to his easel under the trees when he wanted to work. The masterpiece can be seen today in the Musée D'Orsay and its size may surprise you when you imagine it being carried here from rue Cortot. Renoir's friend Henri Rivière, who appears in the painting, describes how the canvas often almost flew off, "like a kite", whilst it was being transported.

Monday evenings at Le Moulin de la Galette

had a different atmosphere entirely. This was the night that local pickpockets, petty criminals, prostitutes and pimps mingled with revellers. Fights would sometimes break out, and trouble often spilled on to the street. Respectable society would not be seen there on Monday evenings, unless it was for the frisson of mixing with the edgier and more dissolute inhabitants of Montmartre.

Confusingly, the Moulin de la Galette was actually the collective name for two windmills on the same site. The Radet, which was restored and moved to its current position on the corner of rue Lepic, was a later edition, built in 1717, whereas the ancient *Blute Fin* was first mentioned as far back as 1622.

A miniature windmill sits on the gravestone above the body of the brave miller, Debray, who was butchered by the Cossacks. His wife cut him down from the sails, and hid his body until she could transport it, secretly, to the Cimetière du Calvaire, where it rests today.

Entrance to Moulin de la Galette on rue Lepic

26. Le Moulin Rouge

The Moulin Rouge

On the site of the White Queen Ballroom, Oller and Zidler opened the Moulin Rouge on 5th October 1889. In the gardens, monkeys roamed free, a huge wooden elephant with movable flanks contained an orchestra and on a stage Moorish dancers performed. Cha-U-Kao, Jane Avril, and particularly the 'realistic quadrille', a teasing dance by La Goulue, ensured that the establishment, immortalised by the canvasses and posters of Toulouse-Lautrec, was a considerable success. On the 3rd January 1907, the mime 'Dream of Egypt' provoked a resounding scandal. With her lover, 'Missy', disguised under the obvious anagram of Yssim, Colette, draped in light veils, took the leading role. Her former husband, Willy, co-author of the piece, was booed out of the room.

Enterprising businessmen Messrs Joseph Oller and Charles Zidler transformed the seedy White Queen dance hall in 1889, creating a new venue where all classes mixed freely in a heady atmosphere of abandon and exuberance. Their showmanship is evident in the acquisition of a huge wooden elephant, a prop bought from the first *Exposition Universelle* of the same year. On a hidden stage, accessed via a spiral staircase inside one of the elephant's legs, belly dancers performed for a 'men only' audience.

At the Moulin Rouge, the Can-Can was fully enshrined in Parisian culture, having originally been invented in local working-class dance halls around 1830. The dance had scandalised bourgeois society, performed as it was by women often wearing no undergarments. They laid everything bare as they high-kicked the evenings away to the obvious delight of male onlookers. High society initially saw this 'aggressive display of working-class sexuality' as a threat to the social order, and outraged descriptions of the dance appeared in the press. Later the Can-Can was tamed and presented in a more choreographed form at the Moulin Rouge, although there was still a fair amount of bare flesh visible to titillate the audience. The outrageous Louise Weber, *La Goulue*, was a big draw and her provocative dances became

Colette in 'Rêve d'Égypte'

legendary. *La Goulue* or 'The Glutton', was a nickname she acquired for her habit of draining the glasses of men watching her as she swirled past their tables.

Jane Avril, who was elegant, graceful and aloof, replaced Louise as the lead dancer at the Moulin Rouge. She fascinated Toulouse-Lautrec as much as had Louise Weber. He painted her obsessively as he sat drinking night after night in the dance hall. He also depicts the clowness Cha-U-Kao in a large yellow tutu. Lautrec's pictures of the dancers at the Moulin Rouge were to become his most famous and widely collected works.

The incident described on the plaque involving Colette, by then a famous writer, was one in which she enacted an amorous scene with 'Missy' – actually Mathilde de Morny, the Marquise de Belbeuf – her then lover. The performance of *Rêve d'Égypte* (Dream of Egypt) involved Colette dressed as a mummy, whose bandages were provocatively removed by Missy, herself dressed as a male

archaeologist. Once unwrapped Colette kissed Missy passionately. Enraged that the family name was being associated with such a spectacle, Missy's brother bought a mass of tickets for the performance and invited his Jockey Club friends to attend. Whilst on stage, the two women were insulted and heckled so raucously that all involved in the performance fled. They locked themselves in the ticket office for safety until the police arrived and dispersed the crowd.

'Willy' was the nickname of Henri Gauthiers-Villars, who organised the event, Colette's first husband and many years her senior. He had begun to pursue her when she was just sixteen. A literary rogue, he passed off Colette's early writings as his own.

The Moulin Rouge has endured in the popular imagination as the epitome of Parisian cabaret nightlife. The beautiful dancing girls remain, but now there are also magicians, singers and tiny Shetland ponies with feathered head-dresses to delight the audience.

The garden at the Moulin Rouge, 1889

27. Le Parc d'artillerie de Montmartre

The Artillery Park of Montmartre

March 1871, and the atmosphere in the capital is explosive. The sufferings of the previous five-month siege, and the humiliation of defeat, have added to general resentment at the blunders of the Monarchist majority in the Assembly, which was recently set up in Versailles. The 18th March dawns and the army, under the direction of Thiers, attempts to seize 227 cannons belonging to the National Guard. Ill conceived and poorly equipped, the attempt fails. The crowd sides with the troops, who disarm their officers. By 9.00 am the Government has lost control and the Central Committee assumes power. From patriotism and revolution, the Commune is born.

Simmering tensions surfaced during the days preceding the Commune. In the wake of France's humiliating surrender to the Prussians, Parisians who had been armed in order to defend the city against the invading army, formed the Federation of National Guards – also known as the *Fédérés*. There were several rowdy demonstrations provoked by rumours that the publicly-funded cannons were to be confiscated. A jittery government, who had witnessed widespread strikes and revolutionary meetings during 1868-70, were anxious about the number of weapons still in the hands of the working-classes with a mood of insurrection in the air.

Events suddenly began to gain momentum. A man called Vincenzoni, suspected of spying, was brutally lynched and several artillery depots were raided. The 'people's' cannons were taken by the Fédérés to safety from place de Wagram in the 17th arrondissement and rolled in convoy up the hill to the safety of The Field of Poles, where Sacré-Cœur now stands.

In the light of these tensions it was perhaps unwise for the head of the government,

Adolphe Thiers, to side with the landlords, who had returned to Paris after the Siege, and begun demanding rent in arrears from the battered population. His decision infuriated the people. When the government troops of the 88th Regiment finally arrived to seize back the cannons at 3.00 am on March 18th, there was no mood for co-operation.

The Fédérés guarding guns were caught by surprise and, without warning, one man, Germain Turpin, was shot by government troops in a sudden volley of gunfire. As he lay bleeding he was tended by Louise Michel **(32)** and other local women, who tore their clothes for bandages. In the confusion Louise Michel saw an opportunity to slip away unnoticed. Running down the hill shouting, "Treason!" she summoned help from the slowly awakening townsfolk.

Due to an astonishing lack of planning, General Lecomte, who commanded the 88th Regiment that day, failed to provide the teams of horses needed to drag the captured guns away. During the delay his young, inexperienced troops were surrounded by

The Field of Poles

women, who appealed to their consciences. They gave the soldiers beer and gradually singing broke out. A carnival atmosphere developed, and Lecomte felt his authority evaporate.

Dr Georges Clemenceau arrived and desperately tried to treat the wounded Turpin, begging General Lecomte to transfer the young man to a hospital. Lecomte refused and in the midst of increasing chaos ordered his troops to fire into the crowds three times. The 88th

Regiment refused, turning their rifles upside down in defiance. Lecomte was dragged from his horse by a furious crowd and taken to the National Guard headquarters at Château Rouge **(15)**, before being transferred to rue de Rosier, where he met his fate **(9)**.

Forced into a humiliating retreat the authority of the National Assembly was shattered. By the next day the people of Paris had seized control of their own destiny and the Commune was born.

Mutiny outside the Town Hall, place des Abbesses

28. Le Passe-Muraille

The Man Who Walked Through Walls

"In Montmartre there lived an excellent fellow named Dutilleul who possessed the remarkable gift of being able to walk through walls with perfect ease." A modest third-class employee in a ministry, he discovered this strange talent by chance, and first used it to drive an assistant director, who had been showering him with insults, quite mad. Following a series of profitable burglaries, in the guise of the Lone Wolf, he gave the Director of La Santé prison the slip, since the man was quite powerless to guard a prisoner who simply went out to lunch and calmly called him to settle the bill. However, our hero was undone by love, sealing him inside a wall after a night of passion. Since then 'on certain echoing winter nights in rue Norvins' only the chords of a guitar played by the painter Gen Paul 'penetrate to the heart of the stones like drops of moonlight'. So it was that in 1943, on an irreverent flight into fantasy, Marcel Aymé's storybook brought joy to many oppressed hearts, and dismissed with a simple tap of his magic wand, the tedium of everyday life.

Imagine discovering that you could walk through walls. Dutilleul, a mild-mannered civil-servant, starts with the best of intentions but soon his extraordinary gift brings temptations too hard to resist: to walk into any bank and help himself, to walk out of any prison that tried to hold him, and to have an affair knowing he could always escape discovery. His downfall came when he finally took the pills his doctor had prescribed for this strange condition. As he walked through the wall that night to meet his lover, he felt an unusual sensation of resistance. As he left, the sensation was even stronger. He never made it back through the wall, and remained there, trapped in the stone forever more.

Marcel Aymé

Marcel Aymé's story of the hapless Dutilleul has delighted generations of French readers with its flight of imagination and gentle humour, elements which typify his writing. His work has found a new audience in recent years as interest in the literary genres of Magical Realism and the Fantastic has increased. He is now recognised as one of France's foremost short-story writers.

Le Passe-Muraille, which appeared as the title of a collection of short stories, was written in 1943 during the Nazi occupation. Fantasy stories had great appeal at that time, since the occupying German censors were less likely to object to their content. In another story, *La Carte* (The Life-Ration), Aymé comments on living conditions in a country under strict rationing. He imagines the system extended to life itself, with each person given a ration card restricting number of days per month they were allowed to exist, according to their 'usefulness'.

Le Passe-Muraille has been made into two films, a television production and a musical. Dutilleul is immortalised in rue Norvins, where Aymé lived, by the extraordinary bronze sculpture that emerges from the wall. It was created by the artist and actor Jean Marais.

"One day, the associate director burst into his closet brandishing a letter and bellowing, "Rewrite this stinking letter! You will rewrite this appalling piece of drivel which is dishonouring my department!"

Dutilleul tried to protest, but Monsieur Lécuyer, in a thunderous voice, called him a hidebound cockroach and as he left, he took the letter he had in his hand, crumpled it up into a ball, and threw it in his face. Dutilleul was modest but proud. He sat alone in his closet, steaming, when suddenly he had an inspiration. He rose from his chair and entered the wall which separated his office from that of the associate director. He was careful to move only partway through the wall, so that just his head emerged on the other side. Monsieur Lécuyer was seated at his work table, his ever-twitching pen shifting a comma in the text an employee had submitted to him for approval. Hearing a quiet cough in his office, he looked up, and discovered to his unspeakable alarm the head (just the head) of Dutilleul stuck to the wall like a hunting trophy. What's more, the head was alive. It looked over its pince-nez glasses at him with deepest hatred. And then it began to speak.

"Monsieur," it said, "you are a hoodlum, a boor, and a spoiled brat." Gaping with horror, Monsieur Lécuyer couldn't take his eyes off this apparition. At last, tearing himself out of his chair, he leapt into the corridor and raced to the closet. Dutilleul sat in his usual place, pen in hand, looking perfectly peaceful and industrious..."

Extract, Le Passe-Muraille

29. Le Sieur Chapelle

Squire Chapelle

Claude-Emmanuel Luillier was born in 1629 in La Chapelle, the son of Marie Chanut and a treasury official named François Luillier, by whom he was legitimised in 1642. Brought up in the name of his home village, he achieved literary fame after the publication of his poems, and particularly for a story in verse and prose 'Journey to Provence' in 1663. A follower of Gassendi from 1641, after college he was a friend of Moliere, Racine, La Fontaine and Boileau. Reproached by the latter for his hedonism he retorted, "You? You're only drunk on your poetry!" Sought in all the best circles, this challenging but loyal companion and unassuming scholar was, in 1686, bestowed the epitaph: 'To his pleasures faithful ever, here lieth Chapelle the clever'.

Chapelle, for whom the epithet *enfant terrible* might have been specially coined, was a friend and confidante to all the poet-stars of the century. Born in the village of La Chapelle to the east of Montmartre, he attended the famous Jesuit Royal College established by Henry IV in La Flèche. Chapelle's father François Luillier, a senior figure at the treasury in the Metz Parliament, asked the brilliant physicist and philosopher Pierre Gassendi to teach his son. Before long Luillier's home became an Gassendian hothouse for the sons of local noblemen, including Cyrano de Bergerac, Molière and Boileau. Chapelle and his group were strongly influenced by their libertine tutor, and went on to form a deep bond of friendship.

Chapelle's excesses in drinking and partying became legendary. He and his friends formed the White Cross Club, named after their favourite tavern. One drunken night, when they were all bemoaning their misfortune in love, they decided as a group that the pain of their broken hearts was too much to bear. Almost too drunk to stand, they all swore to throw themselves into the Seine to teach their lovers a lesson. As they set off to commit collective suicide, Molière quietly suggested that 'such a plan should really be carried out at daybreak', for maximum poetic impact. His friends agreed, but by morning their sore heads meant that the plan was forgotten.

In the 18th century the term 'libertine' became associated with erotic writing or behaviour, but in the 17th century it was more concerned with the philosophical freedom to think, speak, write and act in any way, without fear. Aside from their excesses in wine, gambling and gastronomy, Chapelle and his libertine friends attempted to redefine literary form by blurring the boundaries between genres. They sometimes denied their stories a conclusion or fragmented the narrative, making it hard to follow. Chapelle was chiefly celebrated for his challenging blend of poetry,

C H A   **[335**

Chapelle and faddle, and to fupply the place of the academy po
Chaplain. faddles, which have no ftirrups to them. lic
    CHAPELLE (Claudius Emanuel Luillier), the cu
natural fon of Francis Luillier, took the name of *Cha-* te
pelle from a village between Paris and St Denys, where th
he was born. He diftinguifhed himfelf by writing
fmall pieces of poetry, in which he difcovered great tu
delicacy, an eafy turn, and an admirable facility of ex- th
preffion. He was the friend of Gaffendi and Moliere; w
and died in 1686. wi
    CHAPERON, Chaperonne, or Chaperoon, pro- ha

Encyclopaedia Britannica, 1797

autobiography, fiction and travel journal in his account of a journey to Provence with his friend François Le Coigneux de Bachaumont. Handily entitled, *"A Curious Historical and Valiant Journey, relating Several Considerable Rarities, which are Beautiful and Remarkable to see about France, and further Gallant Discourse, Speeches and Verses by the Most Beautiful Spirits of this Age"*, it certainly confounded literary expectation. Chapelle's other contributions were mainly short satirical poems. His targets were his parents, the Archbishop, indeed

anyone "less honourable" than himself. He also became embroiled in furious rows with other writers, each publishing more and more scurrilous claims about the other.

An epicurean sought for his wit and good company, Chapelle was courted by nobles and aristocrats, which allowed his excesses full rein. His friends Racine, Molière and La Fontaine, after deciding that Chapelle was too fond of wine, tried in vain to rehabilitate their companion. Luillier's drinking finally got the better of him however and he died in 1686.

CHAPELLE.

30. Le Théâtre de l'Atelier

The Workshop Theatre

As reward for his eyewitness account of the death of the Dauphin Louis XVII, Seveste was granted the concession for the theatres beyond the city limits. Thus he was able to build Montmartre Theatre, opened in 1822. Romantic melodrama, comic opera and operetta would play there throughout the 19th century, until the arrival of the impresario Charles Dullin, who in 1922 transformed the space into Le Théâtre de l'Atelier, or Workshop Theatre. Jean-Louis Barrault would make his acting debut there in 1930. From 1940 to 1973, André Barsacq succeeded Dullin. The façade and the foyer, built in the Romantic style, were listed in 1974, and since 1957 the theatre's location bears the name of the founder, place Charles Dullin (1885-1949).

The founder of this little theatre was actor-comedian Pierre-Jacques Seveste. On 10th June 1817, he was granted special dispensation to build a theatre outside the city walls, by Royal Decree. The architect Haudebourg was engaged to design a small wooden theatre. Seveste's troupe of actors gave it the nickname *Galerius Seveste* (Seveste's Galley) complaining that they felt more like galley slaves than apprentices, with long hours demanded of them for virtually no wages. Seveste replied, with some justification, that he was simply preparing them for the reality of life in the theatre. He himself worked tirelessly, opening another théâtre in Montparnasse in 1829 and managing a third in Grenelle.

Galerius Seveste was renamed in the 1848 uprising. Now in the hands of Seveste's widow and sons Edmond and Jules, it became 'The Montmartre Theatre of the People', but did not flourish, and business dwindled to nothing. But, by 1860, things had picked up again, with the repertoire consisting largely of mainstream

Charles Dullin

melodramas and comedies. Many actors who went on to achieve great fame began their careers in the little theatre.

During the Siege of Paris in 1870, when her people were starving, Georges Clemenceau organised a charity performance of Henry

Murger's one-act comedy *Bonhomme Jardis* at the theatre. He played a trick on the company of actors, substituting real meat and butter for the cardboard props in the dining room scene. The actors were astonished, and the audience yelled 'Don't eat it all, save some for us!'

In 1903, a penniless eighteen year old called Charles Dullin arrived in Paris, and decided to perform at The Lapin Agile **(22)**. He recited poetry by François Villon and his performance was noticed by a theatre director, who gave him his first job. He was soon recognised as a gifted actor. Seventeen years later he was to save Montmartre Theatre from obscurity and establish its reputation. Re-naming it Théâtre de l'Atelier in 1922, Dullin inspired a whole generation of young performers and was described by his friend, the great actor Jean-Louis Barrault as,

"...a mix of youth, excitement, rebellion and purity ...he had this wonderful way of being reborn pure each morning. The more Dullin advanced in knowledge of his art, the more he had the art of ignoring it. He discovered every day and we could see his eyes sparkling with the mischief, amazement and wonder of an obstinate child."

Dullin was a hugely charismatic performer and innovator, favouring the foregrounding of text and actor over lavish set design, commercialism and spectacle. He inspired great loyalty from all who worked with him, and became a towering figure in the theatrical world.

When he needed money to continue his work at the theatre Dullin acted in and produced films, both of which he did very successfully. He starred in sixteen films and, in 1942, appeared as himself in a documentary film about the teaching of drama.

Under his stewardship Théâtre de l'Atelier became the Parisian home of experimental drama. Cocteau, Artaud, Sartre and Pirandello all figured in the listings, while audiences could behold innovative treatment of works by Aristophanes, Shakespeare and Jonson. At the Atelier they believed that there was little point in attending a play unless you were ready to have your perceptions, or even your life, changed in some way.

Today, the Atelier's experimental tradition continues under the energetic directorship of Laura Pels.

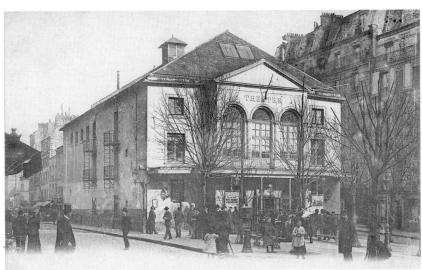

The Montmartre Theatre

31. Les Grands Magasins Dufayel

Dufayel's Department Stores

From 1856 to 1930, Dufayel's offered its clients the dream – within reach and on credit. They would even call at your home to collect monthly payments. But commerce alone was not the point: the emphasis lay, above all, on the triumph of luxury and flair. In 1895, Dalou adorned the cornice with a sculpture entitled, "Progress, and in its train Commerce and Industry". A winter garden allowed you to stroll amongst exotic plants, the high gallery was modelled on celebrated salons, and an orchestra with a vast repertoire accompanied artists from the Opera House. From 1900, the cinema became a natural feature of this programme and on show nights a powerful electric beam was projected upon the town.

Imagine a department store with its own cycle track, where you could try out your bicycle before you bought it; where you could sit under vast glass-roofed halls and hear little birds singing amongst palm trees and fountains; where you could have your feet and hands X-Rayed as a souvenir of your visit, and women were handed a tiny bouquet as they left the building. Such a magnificent department store indeed existed, and its reputation for elegance was such that it soon became a tourist attraction in its own right. No visit to the sights of Paris was complete without a visit to Dufayel's 'Palace of Consumption'. The population of Paris became mass-consumers almost overnight.

The store was the brainchild of M. Georges Dufayel, a great innovator in the new science of retail. He introduced widely available credit, returnable goods, 'sales', and fast stock rotation. He had his own advertising and market research department, and even produced his own trade journal. Profit, surprisingly, was not his main motivation. He came from a humble background, initially working as a clerk for department store owner M. Crespin, and taking over the business when he died. Dufayel had a strong social conscience, and sincerely wished

Interior at Dufayel's. Below, staff uniforms

to see the standard of living improved for the less fortunate. He undertook charitable works for the sick, the poor and the old. Dufayel declared, "I am blamed for my Palace, but who is blaming me? Only the rich and jealous! I myself have known the harsh conditions of life. I have given back to the 'have-nots' courage, confidence and serenity. The humble will thank me."

Running the operation was a complex business. Dufayel installed an underground railway system and warehouses to keep stock rotating efficiently. The building housed stables packed with delivery horses, who even had their own equine swimming pool.

It has been estimated that three out of every seven households in Paris were doing business with Dufayel at one time. Other stores would accept only cash but Dufayel's scheme of cheap credit was very popular. His uniformed money collectors, carrying large bags over their shoulders, were as familiar a sight as postmen. Even Victor Hugo worked as one of Dufayel's credit men for a while.

Now, sadly, only part of Dalou's façade on rue Clignancourt remains. Dufayel died in 1916 and his beautiful shop was stripped of its splendour by subsequent owners.

32. Louise Michel, directrice d'école

Louise Michel, Teacher

"Towards the end of the Empire, I lived with my mother in a small clean and cheerful cottage, where I had set up my first class. It didn't take long before I had enrolled many pupils. I loved these children of Montmartre, kind and open, impish chatterboxes, like little birds..." Born on 29th May 1830 at Vroncourt (Haute Marne), daughter of a squire and a maidservant, Louise Michel began her teaching career in 1853, after rigorous studies. Arriving in Paris in 1856, and faced with child poverty, she discovered her vocation to lead a life of *"propaganda and action"*. As an ambulance worker during the siege of Paris, she served the Commune on the watch committee of Montmartre, in charge of education. She did not hesitate to mount the barricades in May 1871. Once her mother was taken hostage by the Versaillais, she gave herself up, and was sentenced to be deported to New Caledonia. Granted amnesty in 1880, she chose – after other spells in prison – exile in London from 1890 to 1904. From then on she lived from her books and lectures, until her death in Marseilles on 10th January 1905.

Louise Michel, a powerhouse of a woman, was a thorn in the flesh of French authorities for the best part of forty years. She came to Paris as a young teacher and soon became politicised by the events of the fading Second Empire. An innovative elementary teacher, who dared to believe that it was better to interest children than to bore them, Louise Michel found herself at odds with the educational establishment.

She played a key role in the Paris Commune, and was at the centre of events on 18th March 1871 **(27)**. She was president of the Montmartre Women's Vigilance Committee, which was mainly concerned with feeding and clothing the poor during the Commune, and

also oversaw the provision of education. She fought on the barricades, drove ambulances, and was in the Cemetery of Père Lachaise for the last battle of the Communards against the Versaillais. She managed to survive but government troops threatened to shoot her mother in order to make her surrender.

Louise Michel was marched with hundreds of other activists from Paris to Satory Prison in Versailles, a journey punctuated with summary executions of insurgents along the way. At her trial she was defiant, declaring,

"I do not wish to defend myself; I do not wish to be defended. I belong entirely to the social revolution, and I declare that I accept the

responsibility of all my acts. I accept it entirely and without reserve...Since it seems that every heart which beats for liberty has only right to a little lead, I too demand my part. If you let me live, I shall not cease to cry vengeance...If you are not cowards, kill me!"

Louise Michel was a powerful, courageous orator, but the government refused to make her a martyr. The sentence was commuted to deportation.

Arriving in the colony of New Caledonia, she was allowed to resume teaching and stayed there for nine years, teaching the children of the indigenous population and supporting their struggle against French invasion. She became immersed in the Kanak culture and language and fascinated by the plant life she discovered along the coast. Politically, she became increasingly linked to the anarchist cause and, when amnestied in 1880, she returned to a tumultuous welcome from 10,000 Parisians. She immediately joined the anarchist struggle and spent the next five years either leading revolutionary meetings or in various prisons.

For the last ten years of her life, Louise

In National Guard uniform

Michel spent her time between London and Paris, lecturing, participating in political action and even finding time to write a novel. An impassioned revolutionary, she was dedicated to the defence of the weak with an almost religious zeal. Her modesty, bravery and commitment to her beliefs won her the admiration and respect of the French nation.

Louise Michel

33. Mairie de Montmartre

Montmartre Town Hall

On 12th November 1789, the National Assembly decreed the creation of a municipality from each town, village or parish. In March 1790, the commune of Montmartre was born but not without difficulty, as a toll-gate cut the village in two. On 22nd June 1790, Upper Montmartre ratified the election of its own council to be led by Félix Desportes, a fierce supporter of the separation. The municipality of Paris would absorb Lower Montmartre. A native of Rouen, Desportes had lived in place du Tertre since 1788. With patriotic zeal, this gifted administrator converted his own home into the Town Hall for Upper Montmartre and, until April 1793, would establish a strong municipality. On becoming a father in May 1791, he gave three names to his daughter; Flore Pierrette Montmartre.

The division of Montmartre caused controversy within both Upper and Lower communities. Upper Montmartre was more peaceful and rural than Lower Montmartre, having remained essentially unchanged and agrarian in both landscape and economy. Lower Montmartre, by contrast, was becoming more and more alive with cabarets, dance-halls and inns. The inhabitants of Upper Montmartre blamed these new business for the increased taxes levied against the whole area, and resentment started to fester. After some bitter wrangling the National Assembly settled matters and the colourful 27-year-old Félix Desportes de Blinval was elected Mayor in a ballot held in St Pierre's Church **(37)**. He became the first ever Mayor of Montmartre, a totally separate municipality from Lower Montmartre, which was absorbed into the rest of Paris.

Desportes was a dynamic political mover, and caused controversy at every turn of his career. He was admired for his energy, charisma, organisational skills, and not least for keeping order in the community over which he governed despite social unrest.

During the Revolution he entertained all the great insurgent leaders, but simultaneously ingratiated and estranged himself from them with his lavish lifestyle, vanity and self-coined aristocratic title – in fact he was the son of a Rouen merchant. His close friendship with the last Abbess of Montmartre, Marie-Louise de Montmorency-Laval, further damaged his reputation, and he finally found himself under arrest and bound for the guillotine on a trumped up charge, which even his accusers did not seem to believe in. Having spent 117 days in Petits-Pères prison, he takes up the story in a pamphlet he wrote later with typical dramatic flair.

A political chameleon, he lived on to the age of eighty-six, following whichever political movement was in power..

FÉLIX DESPORTES

"I escaped the slaughter only by a miracle. A jailer named Bordeau, who had previously been incarcerated with me in the "Petits-Pères" prison because he had let a convict escape from the prison of Saint-Lazare, and whom I had helped during illness he had caught from being imprisoned… saw me by the light of the torches carried by guards who had come to take us to the Conciergerie; I was at the head of the line of twenty-six prisoners, all chained like myself and destined to mount the same scaffold on the morrow. As was usual, we had been lined up along the wall of a low room, which the prisoners called the mousetrap, because once you entered it, you never came out again except to meet your death.

Bordeau, momentarily dumbfounded by the peril which threatened me, but soon inspired by the memory of the services I had rendered him, proved to me the truth of the old adage: a good deed is never done in vain. It took him no more than a moment to run up to the commander of the gendarmes, whom he seemed to know very well, and talk to him. But imagine my surprise when I saw twenty-six new prisoners, who must have been chosen arbitrarily from amongst the immense number that composed the miserable population of the Plessis Prison. Our chains were transferred to them and the unfortunate fellows, no less innocent than we were, must have perished the next day in our stead…"

Pamphlet, Félix Desportes, 1789

34. Mairie du XVIIIe arrondissement

The Town Hall of the 18th arrondissement

Since 1882, the Paris municipality had been anxious to replace the old Montmartre Town Hall, which had stood in place des Abbesses since 1836. The Prefect of the Seine, Eugène Poubelle, bought a stretch of land in the La place Sainte-Euphrasie, renamed Jules Joffrin in 1895. Time was pressing, with no opportunities for tendering, so the project was entrusted to Marcelin-Emmanuel Varcollier (1829-1895). This former pupil and colleague of Baltard had been the official Town Architect since 1883, and his bold plan submitted in 1888 won over the organising committee. Around a grand glass-topped atrium, the municipal services were gathered within a trapezium-shaped space. Above lay a library, a ballroom and two marriage halls. An eclectic façade, mixing Renaissance-style columns with a Louis XV cornice, led to a five-arched porch, graced with two statues Liberty and Fraternity by Gustave Crauk. The interior decoration of the ballroom, the sculpted and gold-leafed panelling and the star-painted ceiling was the work of the architect Claës. The building was opened on 17th July 1892.

The old town hall of the 18th arrondissement at place des Abbesses was crumbling and in urgent need of a replacement. It is perhaps fortunate in this instance that tendering time was short, since Vacollier's hasty appointment as architect resulted in a truly outstanding municipal building. From the elegant double staircase in the central hall to the gilding, crystal chandeliers and stained glass in the upper Halls, no detail of its design has been overlooked.

One of the local councillors, on approving the lavish Wedding Hall, stated that it was right that it should "...contribute to a sense of luxury that usually accompanies the wedding ceremony which is not always satisfied because simplicity often prevails in town halls..." The result of Claës' wonderful eye for interior design would not disappoint even the fussiest bride.

In the ante-room at the top of the staircase hang two large canvases, *Montmartre* and *Quai de Passy sous la neige*, both by Maurice Utrillo, which he painted shortly before his death in 1955. They are typical of Utrillo's late style, showing his life-long preoccupation with the architecture of the city.

If you pay a visit to the Mairie, it is permitted to walk past the main desk and view the central courtyard; slip up the stairs and peer into the Wedding Hall and Ballroom, and view the Utrillo canvases.

The old Mairie of the XVIII arrondissement

The Ballroom today

35. Monument à la mémoire de Moncey

Monument to the memory of Moncey

This classic of academism commemorates the heroic defence of Paris during the siege of 1841. Amédée Doublemard, (1826-1900), winner of the Prix de Rome in 1854 and 1855. Under the very strict control of the Commission des Beaux-Arts, he was to win another competition organised by the city of Paris in 1863, which led to the erection of this statue. Competing against him was one Carpeaux who put forward a romantic and unstructured piece, a model of which is kept in the Petit Palais. Another competitor by the name of Horeau submitted a plinth topped by a small boat, "tossed on the waves of fortune". Erected in 1869, this monument never had an official opening. The ceremony was planned for 15th August 1870, but was cancelled because France was at war. It presaged a country again threatened with invasion: proud chested and wielding a sabre, Moncey rushes headlong, his left arm outstretched to protect Paris, crowned with towers, and brandishing an imperial eagle. Behind, a student volunteer from the École Polytechnique is dying on the ruins of the barricades. This majestic 14 metre stone allegory is a tribute to a city reshaped by Haussmann and is also considered to be the prototype for all French war memorials.

Napoleon Bonaparte's military daring and vision for France heralded a time of unprecedented confidence. French armies were victorious in wars with Britain, Austria and Russia. But Napoleon's confidence soon led to arrogance. He over-stretched his resources and failed to plan his campaigns, eventually refusing to listen to the advice of his generals at all. Success turned to bitter defeat. His armies suffered huge losses during the harsh Russian winter of 1813, and a year later Austria and Russia's armies approached France's capital once again.

The last battle to defend Paris took place at the Clichy Gate, on 30th March 1814. Marshal Moncey, an experienced and courageous leader, established his headquarters in the local Père Lathuile tavern and orchestrated volunteer fighters as the shooting began. The hastily assembled troops, consisting mainly of young recruits from nearby military and veterinary colleges, and a small number of snipers, were woefully inexperienced. They were also outnumbered and ill-equipped, with not enough rifles for all the men. Some were armed only with pikes.

With the Prussian Army only 500 metres away, Marshal Moncey calmly positioned his snipers in the buildings surrounding the barrier to create an ambush should the enemy break through the barricade. Under heavy fire, women and children worked to build a second barricade to slow down the oncoming troops. Despite fierce fighting all around them, and totally unarmed, these brave defenders continued to add to the barricades using whatever they could find, pulling up flagstones and even bringing furniture from their own houses. The invaders were successfully held back until an armistice was declared at 2.00 am on the morning of 31st March 1814. The defence of the barricades at Clichy went down in history as a supreme act of bravery by all involved, led from the front by Marshal Moncey, and immortalised by Doublemard's iconic monument.

36. Naissance de la Compagnie de Jesus

The Birth of The Jesuits

Already a renowned location for pilgrims since the Middle Ages, this site, supposedly that of the martyrdom of St Denis, had already received some notable visitors; Thomas A Becket exiled to France, the young Charles VI, cured of an early mad fit and followed by his entire court in barefoot procession from Notre-Dame, or Joan of Arc, who had come to pray on the eve of the siege of Paris. On 15th August 1534, after a retreat of penitence and fasting on the hill, Ignacio de Loyola, accompanied by Francisco-Xavier and five other companions, came to ask for the chapel key. During a Mass, at the moment of communion, they proclaimed a triple vow of poverty, chastity and devotion to the salvation of souls. The Society of Jesus was born.

In 275, St Denis, the first bishop of Paris, was beheaded, supposedly on this spot, and the Martyrium was built here to honour his memory. Its popularity as a place of pilgrimage increased in 1133 when King Louis 'The Fat' built the vast Abbey des Dames, covering most of Montmartre's hill. The Martyrium was absorbed into the sprawling Abbey grounds. It was consecrated by the Pope in 1147, and attracted thousands of pilgrims as the legend of St Denis and his miraculous walk **(10)** spread through Europe, via travellers and itinerant court storytellers.

Ignatius Loyola, a Spanish knight, was inspired by a vision he experienced following a serious battlefield injury. He travelled to Paris to found the Jesuit movement, driven by evangelical passion and horror at the changes brought by the Reformation. In this place he and his friends made their holy vows. Loyola asked for a blessing from Rome, and Pope Paul III approved that the Society of Jesus be formed, by Papal Bull in 1540.

The Martyrium

The Jesuits became known as 'the school masters of Europe', with the dictum "Give us a boy and we will return you a man, a citizen of his country and a child of God", at the heart of their philosophy. By the 17th century they had set up more than 500 schools, and the Jesuit teaching model became the basis for many education systems across the world. They were highly effective communicators, using art, theatre and murals to spread their teachings across early modern Europe. However, their wealth and influence over those at the heart of power, seemingly anywhere in the world, caused deep suspicion in some quarters and led to a suppression of the order in the late 18th century. By 1814 they had re-grouped, and now have twenty thousand members worldwide. Keeping pace with the times, and in their tradition of relevant communication, they now offer 'Pray-As-You-Go', a daily prayer podcast.

There was a huge stir in 1611, when a hidden chapel was discovered here, thought to have been constructed by persecuted Christians. The letters **MAR CLEMIN DIO** were discovered, carved into the damp and crumbling rock walls of the secret chamber. This inscription was taken to mean 'Martyr Clement Denis'. Pope Clement was thought to have sent Denis on his mission. By 1794, after Revolutionaries had destroyed many religious buildings, the Martyrium was lost altogether. It remained hidden until 1854.

The Martyrium is now a venue for poetry readings as well as a peaceful place of worship. It is a delight to sit in the quiet and cool for a few moments, away from the tourist bustle, and contemplate the history of this remarkable site.

St Ignatius Loyola

37. Saint-Pierre de Montmartre

St Peter's of Montmartre

From the middle of the 5th century, an early Merovingian church had stood on the site of a temple to Mars. Its ruins were yielded to Louis VI in 1133, re-built as a Benedictine abbey founded by Queen Adelaide of Savoy, and solemnly consecrated by Pope Eugene III on Easter Monday 1147. It is one of the earliest religious buildings of Paris, whose base dates from the 12th century, with some Gallo-Roman additions. Closed to worship during the Revolution, a tower was added above the disused Choir of Ladies, later employed until 1844 for Chappe's optical telegraph. Allowed to deteriorate in the 19th century, it narrowly escaped demolition, and benefited from a radical restoration in 1900.

St Pierre's has faced so many threats during Montmartre's turbulent history it is astonishing that anything remains of it at all. In 1559 the original chapel, which stood within the Royal Abbey, was almost totally destroyed by fire; in 1792, during the religious purges of the Revolution, the Abbey was dismantled, and the current structure built around the choir – the only remaining feature; in 1794 the tower collapsed, having never been built on proper foundations; in 1814 it was commandeered as a barracks for the Cossacks, and in 1871 the church was used as an ammunition depot by the Communards. It was eventually closed due to structural instability, leading to the commissioning of St Jean the Evangelist (2) further down the hill. Yet, despite this litany of disasters, St Pierre's has survived, and remains a focal point and place of worship for the community of Montmartre to this day.

The collapse of the tower in 1794 led enterprising inventor Claude Chappe to build his mechanical semaphore device, *Le Télégraphe*

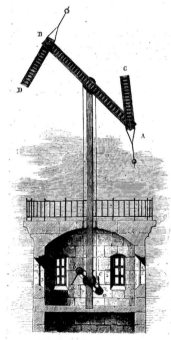

Fig. 19. — Télégraphe de Chappe.

Chappe, on the ruins of the apse. It was a beautifully simple but effective contraption for transmitting information. The *Télégraphe* enabled Parisians to receive news of the Battle of Waterloo within seventeen minutes, beating all other forms of communication exchange by several days. The mechanism, as described in the 1833 *Enyclopedia Britannica of Arts and Sciences*, consisted of,

" *...an upright post, on top of which was fastened a traverse bar, while at the ends of the latter two smaller arms moved on pivots. The positions of these four bars represented words or letters; and by means of machines placed at intervals such that each was distinctly visible from the next, messages could be conveyed through 50 leagues in a quarter of an hour.*"

Tragically, Claude Chappe was seized with a deep melancholia after being falsely accused by a jealous colleague of copying his device from two other inventors, called Hooke and Amontons. Deeply affected by this slur, he committed suicide in 1805. The *Télégraphe* survived until it was destroyed by fire in 1844.

St Pierre's was eventually fully restored. The façade is late 19th century and the three modern bronze doors, by the Italian sculptor Tommaso Gismondi, depict the lives of St John on the middle door, St Denis on the left and Mary, Mother of Christ on the right. They were made in Italy and blessed by Pope John Paul II on 26th March 1980. The four columns that were found amongst the ruins of the Roman temples have been incorporated into the church's fabric.

Saint-Pierre de Montmartre with Chappe's Telegraph

Gazing out across Paris from the top of the Funicular, 1901

Connections Map

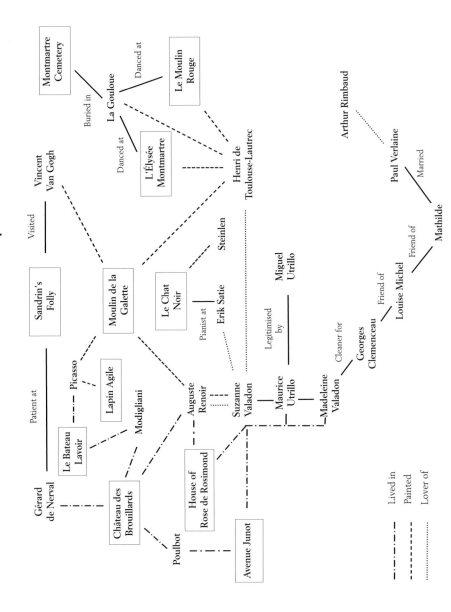

Timeline

1600

1617	Louis XIII becomes king, aged 9
1643	Louis XIV (the 'Sun King') crowned king
1682	Royal court moves to Versailles

1700

1715	Louis XIV dies and Louis XV accedes, aged 5
1774	Louis XVI becomes king
1789	French Revolution, storming of La Bastille
1792	Louis XVI tried for treason and convicted; monarchy abolished
1793	Louis XVI and Queen Marie Antoinette are guillotined in Paris
1793	Revolutionary leader Marat murdered by Charlotte Corday.
1794	Revolutionary leader Robespierre overthrown. Reign of Terror ends
1796	Napoleon marries Rose de Beauharnais – the future Empress Joséphine

1800

1804	Napoleon Bonaparte crowns himself Emperor Napoleon I
1814	Napoleon abdicates and is exiled to Elba
1814–24	Reign of Louis XVIII
1815	Napoleon enters Paris
1815	Napoleon defeated at Waterloo and deported to St Helena
1824	Louis XVIII overthrown by Charles X
1824–30	Reign of Charles X
1830	July Revolution. Charles X overthrown
1830-48	July Monarchy. Reign of Louis Philippe as constitutional monarch
1848	Second Republic declared
1852	Napoleon I's nephew crowned Emperor Louis Napoleon III

1853	Napoleon III commissions Haussmann to redesign Paris
1870	Franco-Prussian War; Napoleon defeated at Sedan and exiled
1870	Second Empire dissolved, replaced by Government of National Defence
1870-71	Siege of Paris
1871	Paris Commune. National Government withdraw to Versailles
1871	Commune defeated. Third Republic declared
1889	Exposition Universelle – Eiffel Tower built
1898 - 1906	The Dreyfus Affair

Opening Times

5	**Maison Eymonaud** – 7 impasse Marie Blanche Open 1st July - 15th September, Mon-Fri 10.00am - 4.00pm
11	**Museum of Montmartre** – 12 rue Cortot Tel: 01 49 25 89 37. Tue-Sun 11.00am - 5.30pm.
20	**Le cimetière Montmartre** – 20 ave Rachel Mon-Fri 8.30am - 5.00pm; Sun 9.00am - 5.30pm
22	**Lapin Agile** – 22 rue des Saules Tel: 01 46 06 85 87 Tue-Sun 9.00pm - 2.00am
34	**Mairie du XVIIIe** – 1 place Jules Joffrin Tel: 01 53 41 18 18 Mon-Fri 8.30am - 5.00pm; Thu 8.30am - 7.30pm; Sat 9.00am - 12.30pm
36	**Martyrium** – 11 rue Yvonne Le Tac Tel: 01 42 23 48 94 Fri 3.00pm - 6.00pm

Acknowledgements

Concept and walk design by Paul Bethel. Concept development, writing and research by Anna Meakin. Translation and editorial contribution by Peter Clare. Image enhancement by Rodolfo Franyutti. Book design by Chris Sims.

Thanks to...

The writer Peter Clare, for generous contributions to chapters; the artist Rodolfo Franyutti for his skilled assistance in restoring damaged images; the artist Chris Sims for book design and creative support; Patrick and Joseph Meakin for their endless patience; the historian Patrick Demer who provided pictures from his superb website on the Franco-Prussian War and Commune www.laguerrede1870enimages.fr; the writer Karen Reshkin for her generosity in allowing us to use extracts from her translation of *Le Passe-Muraille* on page 79; the historian David Hervé, for his kind assistance and highly informative website, www.hervedavid.fr/francais/montmartre.htm; the historian Pascal Ferlicot for generously allowing us access to his private collection of images for Chapter 15, *Le Bal du Château Rouge*, and Chapter 31, *Les Grandes Magasins Dufayel*, at his website www.lagouttedor.net; James for his kind help and encouragement; the novelist Catherine Shaw for her translation of Félix Desportes' pamphlet on page 89; Professor Antonio Gonzáles García for providing pictures from his Spanish website "Toulouse-Lautrec:Photographic Collection; Works, Places and Models"; the genius Steve Essery for technical support; Erik Youngren for exceptional generosity; Claire Phillips for valiant assistance with walks; Claudine Scott for her patience, kindness and teaching; Pip Ward, for proof reading; the archive department of the town hall of the 18th arrondissement; the Museum of Montmartre; Simon Meakin at landmarkmayo.co.uk; .Xavier de Lashwood, for just being there.

Links

www.museedemontmartre.fr – Museum of Montmartre
www.au-lapin-agile.com – official site of the Lapin Agile cabaret. History and music.
www.moulinrouge.fr – official site of the Moulin Rouge. Extended history section and booking
www.musee-clemenceau.fr – Clemenceau Museum
www.hervedavid.fr/francais/montmartre.htm – history and images of Montmartre
www. aloj.us.es/galba/monograficos/lautrec/index.htm – photos of Lautrec, and Montmartre
www.stresscafe.com/translations/pm/index.htm – translations of Marcel Aymé's work
www.laguerrede1870enimages.fr – History of Franco-Prussian War, Paris Siege & Commune

Selected Bibliography

Richardson, John, *A Life of Picasso (Volume II 1907-1917)*, Pimlico, London, 1997; Littlewood, Ian, *Paris – A Literary Companion*, John Murray, London, 1987; Storm, John, *The Valadon Story – The Life of Suzanne Valadon*, Longman, London, 1958; Roe, Sue, *The Private Lives of the Impressionists*, Harper Collins Publishers, 2006; Christiansen, Rupert, *Paris Babylon – Grandeur, Decadence and Revolution 1869-1875*, Pimlico, London, 2003; Thurman, Judith, *Secrets Of The Flesh: A Life Of Colette*, Bloomsbury, London, 1999; Antiff, Mark & Leighten, *Cubism & Culture*, Thames & Hudson, London, 2001; Constantine, H (trans) *Paris Tales: A Literary Tour of the City*, Oxford University Press, 2004; Horne, Alistair, *The Fall of Paris, 1870-1871*, World Books, 1965; Coffin, Judith, *'Credit, Consumption, and Images of Women's Desires: Selling the Sewing Machine in Late Nineteenth-century France'*, French Historical Studies, (Vol. 18, Spring, No. 3), 1994; Murat, Laure, *La Maison du docteur Blanche*, Hachette Littérature, 2001; Chauvat, Dominique & Pédron, François, *D'un Montmartre l'autre*, Les Editions de la Belle Gabrielle 2006; Wiggishoff, J.C, *La Maison Gothique de Montmartre - Le Comte Charles De L'Escalopier, Ses Serres et sa Biblioteque*, Bergerac, 1908; Harvey, David, *Monument and Myth*, Annals of the Association of American Geographers, (Vol. 09, No.3), 1979; Dejean, Jean E, *Libertine Strategies, Freedom and the Novel in Seventeenth-century France*, Ohio State University Press, 1981; *Bulletin de la Société d'histoire et d'archéologie Le vieux Montmartre (Paris), 1906-1910*, BnF; Maupassant, Guy, *Le Masque*, 1889; Boitard, Pierre, *Paris Avant Les Hommes*, Passard, Paris, 1861; Renoir, Jean, *Renoir My Father*, NYRB, New York, 2001; Lissagaray, O-P, *Histoire de la Commune*, transl. Eleanor Marx, 1876;

Picture credits